MW00827692

Kenadi ~
I want you story
For my next Book!
XO
Tina

TINA BLACK

BE

BE AMAZING

Be Amazing!
©2016 by Tina Black

All rights reserved.
No part of this book may be reproduced in any form whatsoever, by photography
or xerography or by any other means, by broadcast or transmission electronically or
otherwise without permission in writing from the publisher, except by a reviewer, who
may quote brief passages in critical articles or reviews.

Published by:
Emerge Publishing, LLC
9521B Riverside Parkway, Suite 243
Tulsa, Oklahoma 74137

TULSA, OKLAHOMA

888.407.4447
www.EmergePublishing.com

Paperback: ISBN: 978-1-943127-28-3
E-book: ISBN: 978-1-943127-27-6

SEL027000 SELF-HELP / Personal Growth / Success

Author Contact:
Tina Black
2950 Lapeer Rd
Port Huron, MI 48060
Tel: 810.987.8118
Email: tina@tinablack.net
Web: www.tinablack.net

Designed by Karen Wilks
Printed in the United States of America

ATTENTION: ORGANIZATIONS and CORPORATIONS
Bulk quantity discounts for reselling, gifts, or fundraising are available.
For more information, please contact Tina@tinablack.net.

20% of the proceeds from this book will go to the nonprofit Andrew Gomez Dream
Foundation, which provides educational support to cosmetology students and
graduates and partners annually with other select charities to jointly raise funds.

DEDICATION

I dedicate this book to all of the Paul Mitchell future professionals and staff members who have asked me through the years when I've taught my success classes, "Do you have a book?" You truly inspired me and gave me the courage to write this book.

ACKNOWLEDGMENTS

This book would not be possible without Jesus Christ, my savior, who gave me life, meaning, and purpose.

My husband, Bryan, who believes in me, supports me, and encourages me to live my dreams.

My kids, Brianna and Justin, who mentor me and make me so proud to be their mom.

Winn Claybaugh, my partner and very first business mentor, who inspired me to become a motivational speaker.

The John Maxwell Team, who gave me the tools for personal growth.

My book coaches, Gail Fink and Kathy Wheeler, who helped me stay focused on getting this book completed.

CONTENTS

PEOPLE ARE TALKING ABOUT
BE AMAZING!

It is very seldom that you come across a person in your life who is pure light. Tina Black is a shining example of personal, professional, spiritual, and financial success. That is why I plead with everyone to not only read this book but to study and cling to every word. Tina's success in all aspects of her life has served as a road map to helping me reach my potential. I truly believe that this mentality, when applied, can change business as we know it.

– Kelly Cardenas, Salon Owner

I've had the pleasure to share the stage with Tina and have the privilege to call her a friend. She is a tenacious leader with a heart for people. Tina is an inspiration to many through her wisdom and rich life experience. I highly recommend reading this book!

– Shelly Aristizabal
Author of *This Is Your Year to Design and Live the Life of Your Dreams*

FOREWORD

I FIRST MET TINA BLACK 15 years ago, along with a group of individuals who were all pursuing the opportunity of becoming Paul Mitchell School owners. We knew back then that we were looking for candidates who were different than what most companies might be looking for. Without getting into details, we turned down quite a few candidates who showed up with millions of dollars, simply because they did not possess the passion or commitment for leadership, giving back, making a difference, and changing lives. Yes, the amount of money in their bank account was secondary to what we wanted to create.

In this group was Tina Black. She stood out, mostly because she wanted to stand out. She knew something great was coming, and she wanted to be a part of it. Of course, we said yes to Tina.

As part of the training and preparation, we challenged our school leaders in many ways, including changing their health and wellness habits by becoming nonsmokers (Tina was already a nonsmoker, thankfully), losing weight if necessary, and committing to whatever they needed to become true mentors. We had many other lessons and requirements of our new partners, but one in particular was one that truly challenged the group: to become a motivational speaker. Why? Because the best leaders, teachers, and mentors are also great communicators and storytellers. When you can move a group of people with your words, you engage their hearts and minds to get the best performance. I know this challenge freaked Tina out, as it does most people. According to the book of lists, people's number one fear is public speaking, and their number two fear is death by fire! (Yes, people would rather die in a fire than speak out in public!)

As I've since learned about Tina, she is up for any challenge. If she is properly loved, educated, and supported, get out of her way. My idea was that our school leaders would take it upon themselves to become the motivational ambassadors within their own schools, but that wasn't enough for Tina. When my book *Be Nice (Or Else!)* came out, Tina became the ambassador of that message and formed BE NICE teams not only in her schools, but in every other school in our network. She then took the BE NICE message into local high schools. When we partnered with anti-bullying expert Dr. Sue Swearer and the University of Nebraska–Lincoln to co-create an anti-bullying curriculum, Tina became the biggest advocate, voice, and promoter of that curriculum. When we partnered with Bright Pink to raise awareness and educate young women to be proactive about their breast and ovarian health, Tina not only invited the training into her own schools, she became the first leader in our network to become a Bright Pink Education Ambassador. When we launched our yearly Paul Mitchell Schools FUNraising campaign, which to date has raised and donated over $15.2 million to a variety of charities, Tina made sure that her schools would be the top fundraisers year after year. When we asked our leaders to seek training outside of our network, Tina immediately signed up with another organization and became a top trainer in their world, recruiting many people to join with her.

I could go on and on with these sorts of examples. Bottom line: Tina Black LIVES what she shares in this book. I know firsthand that none of it came easily or naturally to her. She placed herself in uncomfortable arenas to work through the fear, study the curriculum, gain the knowledge, and elevate her standard of living as a mom, wife, friend, and human being. And the awesome part of this story is that she has recruited anyone and everyone to join her. It does not get better than that.

Yes, I love Tina Black, and I also respect her with all my heart.

— Winn Claybaugh
Dean and Cofounder of Paul Mitchell Schools
Author of *Be Nice (Or Else!)*

ARE YOU READY TO
BE AMAZING?

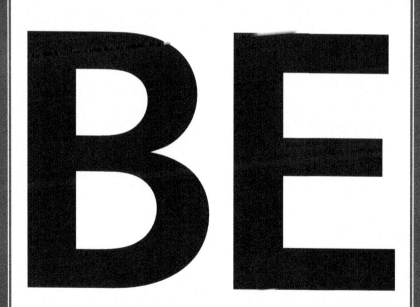

I REMEMBER IT as clear as day. I was 16 years old, sitting in my parents' library, writing a letter to each of my siblings (Tom, Cyndi, Jim, and Linda), letting them know how I felt at that moment because I planned on ending my life that day. This is hard for me to admit, even as I write this book, because not one of them knows about that letter. I never would have dreamed that someday, when I was almost 50 years old and a corporation owner, my story would play out to help so many people.

Over the years, my story evolved into a motivational speech and became the basis of a website (www.tinablack.net) where people like me can tell their stories and help change and shape lives as I have had the honor of doing these past 17 years.

The people in those stories have at least one thing in common: they know how to have ice in their veins.

I learned that phrase from my son, Justin.

ICE IN YOUR VEINS

Stop having a pity party.

When Justin was in high school, he said something really profound, something that would change my world forever. He said, "Mom, after I made a bad play at football practice, one of my coaches told me, 'Hey Justin what's the matter with you? You have to get ice in your veins!'"

Having ice in your veins means that when you make a mistake, you can shake it off, stop having a pity party, forget what you did, and move on.

A year after that conversation with his coach, Justin received a full scholarship to the University of Northern Iowa as a quarterback. You'd better believe he had learned how to have ice in his veins.

What I didn't realize when he told me that story was that I, too, needed ice in my veins. I needed to shake off my mistakes and move on. I needed to learn what bestselling author and keynote speaker Jon Gordon meant when he said,

"Adversity is not a dead-end, but a detour to a better outcome."

If you need ice in your veins and you're looking for tools that can help you with your pity-party days, you'll find them here. This book contains the success strategies I've learned not only from my childhood but also from my newly found leadership and life-strategy training. These strategies can help you reach your dreams. Even more important, they can help you Be Amazing!

DO YOU KNOW THE STANDARD?

Tina, when you are weak, I am strong. I'm your mentor.

What does success mean to you? I've pondered this question for years. At over 50 years old, married more than 30 years, and the mother of two adult kids (Justin and Brianna), I've finally figured out what success means to me.

Success is what my husband and my kids say about me.

Eventually, it'll be what my grandkids say about me.

When my kids were teenagers, I had a terrible dream. In my dream, I thought, *What if my kids took a lie detector test and were asked, "Tell me about your mom, the good and the bad.'* I woke up breathless, panicked, and thinking, *NO!* I didn't like what I'd heard. I asked God right then and there to help me be a better wife and mother. I will never forget the words he told me that day:

"Tina, when you are weak, I am strong. I'm your mentor."

This has proven to be true. God has been my mentor. He has shaped me, my life, and the example I set for my children. He has also provided many mentors to help me along the way; you'll meet several of them in this book.

WHAT'S YOUR WHY?

One night during my son's first year of college, he texted me and asked,
"What's your WHY, Mom?"

I immediately texted back,
"To change people's lives."

Then I texted him again and asked,
"What's your WHY?"

He texted back:
I don't have a comeback story; I was raised by well-off,
successful parents. My WHY is I KNOW THE STANDARD. I
watched my mom wake up every morning with a smile on her
face and run three successful businesses with every ounce
of energy and passion. I watched my dad with a doctorate
degree rake leaves until dark, pour cement in Haiti,
and build homes and properties. He led a law practice, a
family, and served in every possible way, EVERY SINGLE
day. I know the standard. I've sat on a million-dollar
jet with a billionaire who was once homeless. I know the
standard. I've seen it firsthand. I've watched my savior
come into my life and love a sinner. He carried a cross
so I could have freedom and peace. Shame on me if I take
what I have for granted. The standard has been set to
give this life everything I have in my being. Success is
possible. I've seen it. I know the standard.

I knew the meaning
of success.

Those words from my son humbled me. I sat there in tears that night, just thanking God.

After all those years of worrying and prayer, on that night I felt blessed. That was all. Blessed. I knew the meaning of success.

That memory replays in my mind whenever I think of balance and success in my life. As I reflected on it while preparing to teach about balance at a Paul Mitchell School, I wrote the core of the speech I mentioned earlier.

That speech continues to be a living, breathing document on www.tinablack. net, along with interviews with people I've met and now see as my mentors. The speech also forms the foundation of this book, which serves as a workbook for the success class I teach across the country. Both the book and the website are filled with stories of the amazing people who have come and gone or stayed in my life. If you're willing to read the stories, utilize the workbook, and apply the lessons, they can contribute to your success, too.

Don't quit!

When you're having one of those pity-party days and thinking you want to quit, go to my site and read one of the success stories. Watch one of the interviews. And remember:

Don't quit! Get ice in your veins.

That's my legacy and what I hope to give to you as you read this book. Maybe one day you, too, will add your story.

7 STEPS TO SUCCESS

Being successful may not be easy—it requires work and commitment—but it's actually quite simple. That may sound like a contradiction, but the secret to success begins with seven simple steps. Are you ready? Here you go ... on to your AMAZING success!

S – STALK VISIONARIES

U – UNDERSTAND YOUR VALUE

C – CHOOSE YOUR FOCUS

C – CHANGE THE CHANNEL

E – EXAMINE YOUR HEART

S – SOW AND GROW

S – STOP MAKING EXCUSES

1

STALK VISIONARIES

How far are you willing to go?

THE FIRST "S" in my success formula stands for "stalk visionaries." My partner and good friend Winn Claybaugh taught me this.

Winn is the dean and cofounder of Paul Mitchell Schools, the author of *Be Nice (Or Else!)*, and the host of a monthly interview series called MASTERS Audio Club. I remember him telling all of us Paul Mitchell school owners that he was a "motivational speaker junkie," meaning that he used to stalk his favorite speakers until they knew who he was. Little did Winn know ... that was all the inspiration I needed to stalk him and my other business partner, John Paul DeJoria, the chairman and cofounder of John Paul Mitchell Systems.

Yes, Winn was the first person I stalked. And because of Winn my life will *never* be the same. Winn opened my eyes to take risks. Boy, did he ever! You see, I'm a small-town girl from Milford, Michigan, and I was a dental hygienist for 18 years. Now I'm a motivational speaker, author, salon owner, and the owner of multiple Paul Mitchell Schools (with dreams of opening more schools and salons). Who would have thought that would be possible? Thank you, Winn Claybaugh and John Paul DeJoria, for believing in me. If you only knew what you've done for my family and me.

How about you? How far are you willing to go?

Would you be willing to take a mentor to coffee or lunch to get inside his or her head? Would you be willing to find someone who's already doing what you want to do and *stalk* that person—in a good way?

20 SECONDS OF COURAGE

Do it afraid.

I was listening to one of Winn Claybaugh's MASTERS interviews featuring Bright Pink founder and CEO Lindsay Avner. She reminded us listeners of a line from the movie, *We Bought a Zoo*. The message was:

"All you need is 20 seconds of insane courage."

That line reminds me of one of my mantras: Do it afraid. I think of all the times I was afraid to speak to one of my mentors. I'll never forget, in 2005, when Winn invited me to travel with him on John Paul DeJoria's private jet to attend some Paul Mitchell Schools' grand openings. I was so scared to go on that flight—excited but scared—and I did it anyway. I did it afraid.

One evening during dinner on that trip, I found myself sitting with John Paul and Winn, the two biggest mentors in my life. I had thought, *Wow, if I could just sit next to them*, and boom, there we were, Winn on my left and John Paul across the table. John Paul asked where my next school would be and the rest is history.

What if I hadn't "done it afraid"? How about you? As Lindsay Avner reminds us, all you need is 20 seconds of insane courage. Next time you're face to face with your mentor, tell yourself over and over, "20 seconds of courage, 20 seconds of courage." You never know what could happen.

WHATEVER YOU'RE AFRAID OF, YOU SHOULD DO NEXT

If stalking visionaries sounds scary to you, please consider something I learned from my dear friend and associate Sarah Kobeski. Years ago, this lovely mentor taught me another wonderful mantra: "Whatever you're afraid of, you should do next!" I've repeated that mantra to myself over and over since then, and it has helped me immensely in many tense situations such as speaking in front of new groups of people, tackling tough conversations with my family or staff, pressing on toward my goals, and getting up the nerve to stalk visionaries.

Fear looks us in the face on a daily basis, doesn't it?

If not, then we're not stretching ourselves to God's potential in our lives.

EXERCISE:
DO NEXT

Try this experiment. Ask yourself:

Q. What are you afraid of accomplishing?
A.

Q. What do you long to do?
A.

Q. What dreams and goals have you always wanted to accomplish but never have?
A.

Q. What are you afraid of?
A.

Q. If this year were going to be your best year ever, what would you want to accomplish?
A.

DO NEXT: Write down the single biggest thing you're afraid to do right now. What do you fear right now? Which mentor are you afraid to approach? Which visionary do you want to stalk? Whatever you fear, you should do next.

IF YOU'RE NOT FAILING, YOU'RE PROBABLY NOT SUCCEEDING

How far am I willing to go with this?

I've discovered that if you don't put yourself out there to fail, you will probably never succeed. Fear of failure prevents us from reaching our God-given destiny. God doesn't call us to be successful; he calls us to be faithful.

Putting myself out there has always been easy for me in business because I have such a supportive husband. He's always been there when I fell … literally! When we met more than 28 years ago, he wanted to take me downhill skiing. Mind you, I had never set foot on anything other than a sled before that point in my life. I remember the first big hill I went down: I cried the entire way down, fell at least a dozen times, and said every cuss word known to man. (I do that when I get scared.) At the bottom of the hill, Bryan picked me up like a rag doll and said, "Look up that hill. You made it down without one broken bone!" I looked through my tears, smiled, and thought, "Hmm, he's got a point!" So what did I do? I took the chairlift back up the hill!

When I ponder the quote that I teach around the country—"Whatever you fear you should do next," or as I say now, "Do it afraid"—I ask myself if I have done that consistently in my life. The answer is a resounding NO! I fear skydiving and wouldn't ever think of doing it. I fear snowboarding, and this old body will NEVER get on a snowboard. I would never subject myself to the pain of repeatedly falling or risk breaking any of my bones.

So I ask myself, *How far am I willing to go with this?* I've decided that as long as it's not life threatening or painful, I will push myself to take more risks.

GET OUT OF THE BOX

Being "in the box" means you'll believe it when you see it. This limiting belief will strangle your dreams. Getting "out of the box" means looking, behaving, and believing differently than that.

It means you don't believe it only after you see It, you believe it before you see it.

The dictionary defines "normal" as conforming to a standard, or conformity. Since most people are "in the box," that makes it the normal way to behave. But who wants to be labeled "normal"?

Being normal follows the 80/20 rule. In 1906, Italian economist Vilfredo Pareto noticed that 20 percent of the people in Italy owned 80 percent of the land. On further research, he observed that the 80/20 relationship applied to other areas as well. Eventually, the principle that 20 percent of the causes are responsible for 80 percent of the results became known as the Pareto principle or the 80/20 rule.

I've seen the 80/20 rule with my very own eyes. Being in the hair industry since 1998, I've watched the majority of my staff and students make "normal" choices, or stay comfortable instead of achieving their goals. Only a few get outside the box and reach for their dreams.

Why are you picking on me?

Winn Claybaugh teaches this philosophy with the Team Vision poster shown opposite. As you can see, it supports the 80/20 rule, showing that only 20 percent of the people in an organization choose to play the role of a visionary.

I have applied this concept not only in my own life but also in coaching my staff and future professionals. When I hear people say, "I can't do that," or "I don't have any money," or "She made me do that," or "Why are you picking on me?" or "Everyone else does it," those individuals come across as resisters or fence sitters. Because I know that such behavior stems from their limiting beliefs about themselves, I then know it is my job to point out their value, potential, and strengths.

My job is to speak life into them and let them do the rest.

TEAM VISION:
The role you choose to play

20% Visionaries
Leaders within the organization who see and support the vision.

50% Fence Sitters
Team members who are not fully committed to the vision.

30% Resisters
Team members within the organization who resist, criticize and undermine the vision.

Based on Winn Claybaugh's *Be Nice (Or Else!)*. Reprinted with permission.

VISIONARY BEHAVIOR

How do visionaries act?

How do visionaries act? What do they look like? Not long ago I heard celebrity life coach Tim Storey use the term "utmost people," which he defined as people who have uncommon plans, uncommon thoughts, and uncommon friends.

That's my idea of a visionary!

In his book, *Be Nice (Or Else!)*, Winn Claybaugh teaches another tool called the Golden Rules. These success tips are the 10 commandments (or in this case, 13) for any business, occupation, or role in life. Look for these habits in other people, and you'll find visionaries worth stalking. Adopt these habits yourself, and you'll soon be part of that top 20 percent!

GOLDEN RULES:
A Code of Conduct

1. Be on time. Always!
2. Always be in a great mood. (Fake it when necessary.)
3. Come to work prepared.
4. Be informed. (Read all memos and information.)
5. Gossip is not allowed.
6. Hold each other accountable (24-hour rule.)
7. Resolve all personal challenges with love.
8. Go to the decision maker with any apparent unsolvable challenges. Use the "Go In Asking" rule.
9. Be knowledgeable, literate, and articulate.
10. Always "look the part" of an impeccable professional.
11. Be professional always.
12. Do not get personally involved with clients.
13. Personal lives remain personal.

Based on Winn Claybaugh's *Be Nice (Or Else!)*. Reprinted with permission.

YOU ARE WHO YOU HANG WITH

"You are the average of the five people you spend the most time with."

Another visionary I stalk, motivational speaker Jim Rohn, famously said, "You are the average of the five people you spend the most time with." Or another way to say it: it's not rocket science that you'll be like the top five to ten people you hang out with. Of course you are who you hang with. I mean, look at married couples: eventually they start looking alike!

I don't know about you, but I am energy sensitive, meaning that the people I hang out with impact my energy level. No one tells it better than another one of the visionaries I stalk, Jon Gordon. In his book *The Energy Bus*, he talks about energy vampires—people who will suck the life out of you, your goals, and your vision if you let them.

When I'm in the room with an energy vampire, I start going negative. But the opposite is equally true:

Give me a positive person and I'm in.

Since I've learned this valuable lesson, I've become very intentional about who I spend my time with, who I hire, and who I keep in my life. I've learned to love those dramatic, issue-filled energy vampires from a distance.

EXERCISE:
MAKE A STALKING LIST

We truly become a product of the people we hang with, so try this exercise to make sure you're headed in the right direction.

Which visionaries could you stalk? List them here:

1.

2.

3.

4.

5.

6.

7.

8.

NOT TO MENTION ...

ANOTHER REASON TO STALK VISIONARIES

Money isn't everything, but I can tell you this: most of the financially successful people I know are positive, happy people—the kind of people I like to be around. I will admit that I know a few wealthy people who've forgotten how to be nice. I just separate myself from them and love them from a distance, too.

At the same time, some of the most successful people I know have very little money. These people are mentors in other areas of my life, such as helping me to stay balanced, which we'll get into in the next chapter.

However, if you want to achieve financial success, you'll want to stalk visionaries in that area and hang around with them. Try the following exercise to see if you're headed in that direction right now.

EXERCISE:
ARE YOU IN GOOD COMPANY?

Make a list of the five people you spend the most time with. Next to their names, write down their yearly income (it's okay to guess). Next, calculate the average of their combined income.

Name	Yearly Income
Name	Yearly Income
Name	Yearly Income
Name	Yearly Income
Name	Yearly Income
	Average

I've heard it said that that's how much you will likely make five years from now. That's good news for some of us. How about you? Do you have some adjustments to make?

When will this pain in my life go away?

Here is what my friend and colleague Shaun Chiodo says about the people he used to hang out with and how they influenced him:

Reflecting back to the people I hung out with when I was in high school and for the next four years after that, I was them. I was sucked into the party life, the bar scene, the late night partying, and sleeping all day, only to do it over and over again and seeing nothing wrong with it because the people I hung out with were doing the same thing. I managed to be arrested multiple times for drinking and driving; I rolled a car 70 feet end over end and walked away, never realizing that God loves to use ordinary people to do extraordinary things. All I thought about was, *When will this pain in my life go away?*

Since that time, Shaun changed who he hangs out with and he is now the successful Director of Operations for three Paul Mitchell Schools. If he can do it, so can you. Shaun now recognizes that God loves to use ordinary people to do extraordinary things, which is key for you to know, too.

GOD LOVES TO USE ORDINARY PEOPLE TO DO EXTRAORDINARY THINGS

One Bible verse that continues to change my life and encourages me to take risks is "I can do all things through Him who strengthens me" (Philippians 4:13). If you don't believe that you can do all things, consider the examples of Noah, Moses, David, the disciples, and so many others who performed seemingly impossible feats because of their faith.

Remember when I told you that I wanted to end my life at age 16? That was such a dark hour in my life. From ages 16 to 18, I merely existed. I made it past my suicidal state but was not living my life with a purpose. I dated one guy after another, played sports, and worked. Those activities kept me going: I became driven, desperately trying to find acceptance through sports and work, both of which I excelled in greatly.

All of that transformed when I was 18 years old and my sister (another mentor in my life) introduced me to life with a belief in God. At age 18, I discovered that I'd been born with a purpose. Life with God was much more fulfilling than life without him. Here I am now, a living, breathing example of God using ordinary people (you can't get much ordinary than me!), which leads us to the next step to success:

Understand your value.

END OF CHAPTER EXERCISE:
BE AMAZING: STALK VISIONARIES

Find a visionary mentor and ask these questions:

What is the greatest lesson you have ever learned?

What are you learning now?

How has failure shaped your life? (Attitude only shows up in failure, not in success.)

Who do you know that I should know? (the greatest networking question to ask)

What have you read that I should read? (personal growth question)

What have you done that I should do?

How can I add value to you? (expresses gratitude)

2

UNDERSTAND YOUR VALUE

When did we stop winning and get into a place of losing?

AT A CONFERENCE, I once heard Pastor Rich Wilkerson Jr. give an amazing illustration about the importance of understanding our value. (You might know him as the pastor who performed the wedding ceremony of Kim Kardashian and Kanye West.) At the conference, Pastor Wilkerson said something along these lines:

Are you kidding me, you don't think you're a winner? How old are you? That many years ago (give or take nine months), you were just a sperm. You were the man (or woman), you had over 100 million friends, Twitter was on overload, and one day you were just chilling with your friends, and you heard there was a race. So you got up to the starting line, you looked up that dark tunnel, you heard the gun go off, and out of 100 million other sperms, you won the race! What are you talking about, you're not a winner? The fact that you are here means you were born with a purpose.

Wilkerson went on to ask: When did we stop winning and get into a place of losing? That's the moment we stopped taking a risk!

DEVELOP A HEALTHY SELF-IMAGE

The Bible reminds us that we are "fearfully and wonderfully made" (Psalm 139:14 NIV) and "We are God's masterpiece. He has created us anew in Christ Jesus, so we can do the good things he planned for us long ago" (Ephesians 2:10 NLT).

On the days when I believe I am God's masterpiece, I am unstoppable. Those are the days I m in the zone." On those days, I don't have to fake it so much; my smile is real and comes easily.

You are God's masterpiece. Do you believe that? Let it sink deep inside. If you're not convinced that you are a masterpiece, this chapter will help. Understanding your value might require you to do some work in three key areas: developing a healthy self-image, increasing your self-confidence, and maintaining balance.

A healthy self-image and understanding your value go hand in hand. Many people, including me, struggle with one particular aspect of their self-image: body image and weight.

As far back as I can remember, I have always been on a diet. Even at 12 to 14 years old, I was so obsessed with diets that I kept journals that mainly focused on my exercise plan and what I ate each day. While most kids were sleeping in on Saturdays, I'd get up at 6 a.m. to go jogging, just to lose a couple of pounds, especially when I thought I had eaten too much the night before. I joke about it now with my friends and family, but they all know I've tried every diet in the universe, from the Atkins diet to the Skinny Bitch diet (which is vegetarian, by the way). I got bored easily! These days, I'm rarely more than 10 to 15 pounds over my goal, but I'm always in the process of trying to master weight loss and my diet.

I know it affects my self-image, and it's not something I like about myself, but here it is: I love food! And when I'm bored, I eat. For me, the solution is a matter of channeling my passion for eating to other passions and finding the balance. I also know that developing rituals leads to success: my time has to be intentionally scheduled so I don't think about food all the time. Being a Team Beachbody coach for the last several years has added accountability to this area of my life.

Most important, I've come to realize that there is more to a healthy self-image than weight and diet.

God thinks every life is valuable, but there were three times in my life when the devil made me think otherwise.

I can't bear to watch.

The first was when I was 16 years old and suicidal. Up until the ninth grade I was bullied repeatedly because of my looks: I was called buck-toothed beaver, and "four eyes" was synonymous with my name. I covered my hurt with a smile and laughter, and I became obsessed with wanting to fit in. It didn't really work; to this day, if someone asks me to watch a bully-related movie or any movie where people hurt other people, I can't bear to watch.

Ask my family: I never watch a scary movie— never!

It has to be romance or comedy; that's it. And when bullying is on the news, I can't watch that, either. When I hear about bullying or abuse I want to open up a home, take all those kids in, and smother them with love. I also still have problems choosing outfits and making decisions about my hair because of lingering limiting beliefs about myself. Fortunately, God sent me a wonderful daughter who is extremely talented in this area and a good friend who shops for a living. I use these limitations to my advantage now. (So there!)

The second instance is something I rarely share with others: during both of my pregnancies, I had a strong desire to die. I honestly understood how people could turn to someone like euthanasia activist Jack Kevorkian, because they felt so sick they wanted to die. For the entire nine months when I was pregnant with both of my kids, I vomited several times a day. There were times when I had to throw up in a garbage can while sitting on the toilet because it was coming out of both ends. (I know this is TMI, but I want you to get the picture.) I would sit

We are valuable!

on the couch and think to myself, *I can't fake happiness anymore. Please, Lord, just let me die.* I cried myself to sleep more nights than I could count, and I was hospitalized for dehydration four times during each pregnancy. It's a miracle that both kids came out perfect when I couldn't even keep my prenatal vitamins down. It got to the point where I only ate foods that I didn't mind throwing up.

The third time I questioned my value happened in 2014. I was diagnosed with a precancerous lesion on my uterus and underwent a full hysterectomy at 49 years old. During my second week of recovery, I had two days of severe depression.

Now I look back on those occasions and know it was the devil trying to steal my joy. John 10:10 says, "The thief comes to kill and destroy, but my purpose is to give them a rich and satisfying life." Did you get that? God wants *you* and *me* to have a *rich and satisfying* life. Meaning he wants us to have *success!* You? Me? Yes! We are *valuable!*

Close your eyes for at least a minute. God loves you with an everlasting joy. Let that sink in.

Do you believe it? Well, to be honest, I don't always believe it, either. I have my ups and downs. But now when I'm having a "down," I know it didn't come from God. I learned a long time ago from author and televangelist Joel Osteen that if I'm having a negative thought it's not from God. In fact, it's quite the opposite. God has given me the opportunity to use my pain to help him in this battle.

As a child, I attempted to shut out the name calling by reading books such as *Little House on the Prairie* and living in a fantasy world of playing house and imagining myself married and living happily ever after. That drove me to the life I live today.

It's amazing but true—what you focus on starts to grow.

As an adult, I have been heavily involved in developing an anti-bullying program with Paul Mitchell Schools and the University of Nebraska–Lincoln. As a result, I now visit elementary, middle, and high schools to share my story and raise awareness to spare others from my pain.

Now I no longer feel useless. My self-image rises and I realize, "Tina, you have value! You've turned your experiences into a message that helps other people. "I am also in the process of developing a team to teach transformational leadership in high schools as well as developing a next-generation team to train leadership and communication skills to the Millennial generation.

Now I just want to help others see what I see and feel the hope I feel. This is my purpose. I know who God has made me to be. As Psalm 139:14 says, "I praise you because I am fearfully and wonderfully made." He doesn't make mistakes.

YOU ARE VALUABLE!
YOU'RE A WINNER!

What will give you the confidence you need to reach your purpose?

Earlier, you met Shaun Chiodo, the operations director of three Paul Mitchell Schools. Shaun understands his value now, but that wasn't always the case.

I did not feel that I had any value. I remember when my uncle stood over me when I was eight years old and told me I'd never amount to anything and I was no better than an ant. Now that drives me forward every day.

Tina says to develop a healthy self-image. I never had the opportunity to do that until I met someone who finally believed in me. Dealing with molestation and being gay at an early age of growing up, I never felt I was given the opportunity to have a healthy relationship with myself. I never saw myself as anything good, even though I had my own house at 20, a great job, traveled and lived the high life. I was still not having a healthy balance. I was out all night, every night drowning away the past. I was choosing to be a victim and not a survivor. I had to develop self-confidence and balance in my life. All are things I did not know until I sat through Tina's success class. Now I use my story to help others.

What will give *you* the confidence you need to reach your purpose? When you reach for your purpose, you'll know it. As one of my other mentors, bestselling author and motivational speaker Eric Thomas, says, "Your passion will wake you." It will also require you to step into the unknown.

ANOTHER KEY:
SELF-CONFIDENCE

The second important key to understanding your value is self-confidence. God wants you to be strong. As Deuteronomy 31:6 says, "Be strong and courageous. Do not be afraid or terrified . . . for the Lord your God goes with you; he will never leave you or abandon you."

When I tell others how low my self-esteem has always been, they are often shocked. That's because, as a young girl constantly being called names, I learned to fake it. I developed a thick exterior but inside I was breaking. For years I cried myself to sleep until I could cry no longer. Those tears eventually dried up. I suppose you would say, as my son says, that I got ice in my veins. This has proven to help me a lot as a business owner. Little do my staff or students know that my heart breaks when someone leaves my business; because of my faith, forgiveness comes easily for me. People may leave, but God has proven that he never will.

Years ago when Winn Claybaugh started the Paul Mitchell Schools, he wrote the book *Be Nice (Or Else!)*. Other than the Bible, it was the first book I'd ever read that completely turned my world upside down. I mentioned earlier that, during one school owner's meeting, Winn announced that all of us owners must become motivational speakers. When I heard those words, I slumped down in my chair, feeling like he was looking right at me, and thought, *No, Winn. I can't! Don't you understand that my self-esteem is too low?*

I could never stand on stage and tell my story!

Will I ever have all the self-confidence I need?

Then Winn said something profound. He said it's easy—just pick one chapter out of his book, something that speaks to you or something you potentially need to work on, and talk about that. Share your feelings about it with your audience. Well, that turned out to be easy, because it seemed like he had written a chapter just for me: chapter 4, "Boost Your Self-Esteem." That chapter became the core of every class I teach.

It started as a 10-minute talk and grew into a 3-hour class.

Another one of my dearest friends and mentors, salon owner Kelly Cardenas, always says, "Act as if" and "You play like you practice." Kelly says we shouldn't have to prepare to be onstage because when we speak, we should talk about what we do every day. He says that when people "speak from the heart," it means they speak from their own experience. That rang true for me: I knew I needed to not only share my story but to also share what I do every day (and what I'm working on).

Winn teaches that those who do the work do the learning, and I agree. The more I teach courses about self-image, balance, and confidence, the stronger I get. Will I ever have all the self-confidence I need? Of course not, but as Winn teaches, I can have fun practicing it—and so can you!

FIND YOUR BALANCE

Will any of us ever be completely balanced and satisfied in every area?

Winn also teaches that we aren't just professional "human doings," we're physical, intellectual, emotional, and spiritual human beings. When we're at work, we don't leave our souls at home.

We need to keep all the areas of our lives in balance.

That was the most profound thing I could ever have read. Since I read those words and started teaching that message in 2004, my life has never been the same.

With this new awareness, I now see my staff, students, and others around me in a completely different way. When they're struggling in their positions or seemingly frustrated, I know they are just out of balance.

Will any of us ever be completely balanced and satisfied in every area? Of course not! Life happens, and sometimes one area requires more attention than the rest. But we can constantly check on these areas, be intentional about staying grounded, and "refill our reservoirs," meaning we can (and must) replenish our energy when it gets drained. After all, we can't give what we don't have. I love it when airline attendants say, "Take your own oxygen first, and then help others around you." How often do we try to help others around us while suffocating for our own air? How can we tell when we're doing that? We get stressed, anxious, scared, and depressed, just to name a few.

Try the following exercise. You might be shocked to see what happens.

EXERCISE:
THE BALANCE WHEEL

Below is a balance wheel with eight areas of life.

In each section, rate your current status using a scale of 0 to 10, with 10 being the highest. Color in the section from the 0 mark up to the mark you gave yourself. What does your wheel look like?

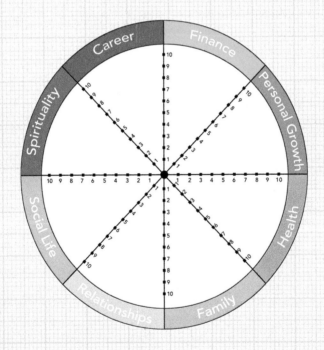

Once you see your balance wheel results, you can make action plans for any areas you want to improve. Once you set up your action plans, commit to being intentional about focusing on each area. My action plans go right into my schedule. I write them down! What you focus on will grow—guaranteed!

VALUES VS. BEHAVIOR

Have you ever noticed?

Paul Mitchell Schools have a great culture piece called Values vs. Behavior. Have you ever noticed that some people will say they value their health but then they'll gorge on cupcakes, coffee, and soda and won't drink enough water? When that happens, their behavior is not in line with their values. Soon their balance wheel becomes unbalanced and needs to be adjusted again.

Over the years I've learned a trick for keeping my self-confidence high: that trick is to never slip on my non-negotiables—the areas I value the most. I've realized that my non-negotiable areas are physical (which fits into the health category) and spiritual (which, for me, falls under personal growth). When I lack discipline in these areas, I don't feel good about myself. My tendency toward anger intensifies, and I feel more anxious or depressed. And trust me, those days have happened too many times over the years to even mention.

Staying in balance would be a constant push and pull if I let it.

As I've mentioned before, I have to be disciplined in these areas by writing them into my schedule. Even though I travel a lot, I stay consistent with my schedule because I know I can't let it slip.

Just pull up your bootstraps and start over.

To save time and make it fun, I've found ways to be creative with my values and behavior, and you can, too. With the help of technology, it's so easy these days. For example, I have a Bible app (YouVersion) on my phone so I can listen to God's word while I'm at the gym. Why just listen to music when I can combine the two? It gets me off to a perfect start and sets the tone for my entire day. If I miss my physical and spiritual workout routine, I have to go into plan B for that day and make sure I get them both in somehow.

It's important to note that when you do slip from your non-negotiables (and you will!), you must quickly forgive yourself. As I always say, just pull up your bootstraps and start over. It's okay!

Now it's your job to identify your non-negotiables.

BE AMAZING:
UNDERSTAND YOUR VALUE

Before you leave this chapter, fill in the balance
wheel, if you haven't done it already, and answer the
values questions on the following page.

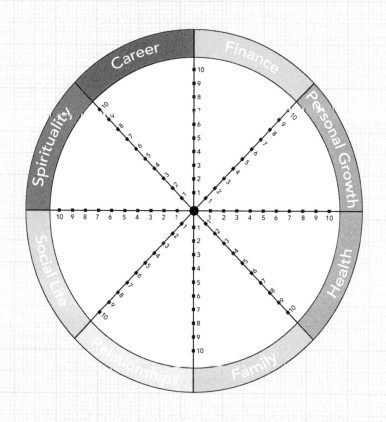

END OF CHAPTER EXERCISE:

BE AMAZING:
UNDERSTAND YOUR VALUE

This life-changing activity came from Christian Simpson, my coaching trainer at the John Maxwell speaking and coaching certification.

1. Think of someone who knows you well, someone you'd go to for advice.
   If they had to describe what you stand for, what would they say? List five values.

_____

_____

_____

_____

_____

2. Now write five values that are non-negotiable in your life.
   Don't think too hard on this.

_____

_____

_____

_____

_____

3. Where do these non-negotiable values show up in your day-to-day life?

_____

_____

4. Which one of these values do you tend to sell out on the most?

_____

_____

_____

Build the discipline to check your non-negotiables daily and commit to making 10 percent shifts to move you toward success. Go ahead, you're worth it!

3

CHOOSE YOUR FOCUS

Do you focus on what you do have?

STUDIES SHOW that the human mind tends to gravitate toward negative thoughts. The Bible tells us, "Be alert and of sober mind. Your enemy the devil prowls around like a roaring lion looking for someone to devour" (Peter 5:8). Knowing this, we have to be proactive.

When you get up in the morning, do you choose to look at everything you don't have? Or do you focus on what you do have? Amazing people understand that we choose our focus. Instead of complaining and getting uptight about the little things that steal our joy—like losing our car keys, getting stuck in traffic, or spilling our coffee—we need to relax and go with the flow. Choosing our focus can help us stop making mountains out of molehills.

Life is too short to focus on the negative!

Choosing to focus on the negative is nothing more than a bad habit. This chapter will help you learn to focus on the positive and set yourself on the Be Amazing path.

PUT YOUR FAITH AHEAD OF YOUR PROBLEMS

Believe me, I can sometimes be the first one to get agitated over those little things. I even get irritated over getting irritated so fast! But Proverbs 16:9 reminds me that the Lord directs our steps. If that isn't confirmation that I need to put my faith ahead of my problems, I don't know what is. That's why "Put your faith ahead of your problems" is one of my mantras now.

How do I put my faith ahead of my problems? For me, it starts first thing in the morning. I've learned that when I'm planning my schedule each morning, I have to be intentional. I remind myself that problems will happen, and I think about what I will do to help overcome them that day. I will not allow them to take my joy! Author and televangelist Joel Osteen says that delays might be the miracles or breaks in our lives. He suggests that we categorize our problems: is it a 5-minute problem, a 5-hour problem, or a 5-month problem? We shouldn't treat our 5-minute problems like they're the end of the world.

Here are a few more great quotes about putting faith ahead of our problems:

- Ephesians 4:23 says to be constantly renewed in your mind.
- Thoughts = Destiny: Thoughts become words, words become actions, actions become habits, habits become character, and character becomes our destiny.
- Romans 8:28 reminds us that "All things work together for good."
- Celebrity life coach Tim Storey says, "Your setback may be your comeback."
- Christian speaker Joyce Meyer says, "When you complain, you remain."

Negative thoughts do *not* come from God. Put faith ahead of your problems, choose your focus, and be intentional about turning negative thoughts around.

AN ATTITUDE OF GRATITUDE

What are you focusing on?

In some cases, choosing our focus might require us to put on a new attitude. Maybe we need to stop being sour all the time and instead choose an attitude of gratitude. The more gratitude we have, even about our challenges, the more joyful we become.

If you've chosen a sour attitude up to now, it's time to stop being a Negative Nancy, Larry Low Rider, Wendy Whiner, or Debbie Downer! (Sorry if one of those is your first name.) The question is, what are you focusing on?

Along those lines, we must even be careful about complaining to close friends and family members.

I catch myself doing that often, and I'm in the process of training myself with this new mantra: Instead of going to the phone, go to the throne.

CHOOSE YOUR FOCUS TOWARD OTHER PEOPLE

Focus on people's strengths instead of their weaknesses.

We all have frustrations—frustrations with family members, friends, our marriage, our parents, our children. If you want to Be Amazing and succeed in life, you have to focus on what you like. Let God change people… and at the same time, it couldn't hurt for you to start praising them for what they're doing right.

I used to have a terrible habit of constantly pointing out what people were doing wrong, and I lost some amazing staff members because of it. Then I discovered the book *Strength Finder 2.0* by Tom Rath, which includes a link to an online assessment that helps users identify their greatest strengths. It also provides each user with a specific action plan for staying in their "strength zone" at all times.

Using this book with the key leaders on my team helped us all understand our value. Each week for one whole year, we'd choose a new action plan based on our individual *Strength Finder 2.0* results. For example, one of my strengths is "achiever," and a suggested action for that strength is to partner with other hard workers and share my goals with them so they can help me get more done.

Now I use this material with all of the staff in my businesses. If I notice someone on my team who seems out of balance or frustrated, we return to this process and get back to their strengths.

It's amazing how much you can lift people up and grow them to be better leaders when you focus on what they do right.

When you focus on people's strengths instead of their weaknesses, you'll be amazed at what can happen to them.

CHANGE YOUR FOCUS ... FAST!

In *Stomp the Elephant in the Office*, best-selling author Steven Vannoy introduced a concept called the Energy Map, which represents every second of every day—100 percent of our energy, time, and potential. Vannoy says we either use our time well by moving toward the "front side," or waste our time by moving toward the "back side."

"When things are tough," Vannoy writes, "most people default to an approach that focuses on problems, what is not working, and who is to blame." Instead, he recommends a more positive, front side approach: focus on our past success by thinking about what is working and what we can learn from our problems and tough times.

We've made this concept a part of the culture in our Paul Mitchell Schools. Instead of vocalizing a negative thought the minute they have one, we encourage our students and staff to say what they like about the situation or to think of an aspect they're grateful for. This simple but in-depth process can help you manage your thoughts and energy any time and any place.

Try this fun little exercise to see how shifting a word can change your energy.

EXERCISE:

CHANGE YOUR WORDS, CHANGE YOUR ENERGY

1. Draw a big circle, and draw a vertical line down the center.

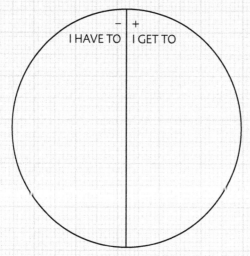

2. On the left side of the circle, draw a minus sign (–) at the top, and write the words "I HAVE TO." Then list all the things you have to do, such as:

Pay bills

Clean my car

Clean my house

Go grocery shopping

3. Now, on the right side of the circle, draw a plus sign (+) at the top and write the words "I GET TO" — and then list those very same things:

Pay bills

Clean my car

Clean my house

Go grocery shopping

Once you switch your thoughts from negative (back side) to positive (front side), your energy shifts and your world will change.

BE INTENTIONAL ABOUT YOUR DAY

Why are some people more successful than others?

If everyone has the same number of hours in a day, why are some people more successful than others? The difference lies in how they manage their time and what they focus on.

In his book *Leadership Gold*, John Maxwell wrote a chapter called "Don't Manage Your Time—Manage Your Life." Maxwell says our days are like suitcases: even though we all have the same size suitcase (24 hours a day), some people can pack more into theirs than other people can.

In other words, some people are better packers!

These days, I'm a pretty good packer but it wasn't always that way. Until my mentor and partner Winn Claybaugh showed us his method of calendaring about four years ago, I used to think, *Oh, I'll remember that, I don't need to write it down* ... but then I'd forget a few important meetings and lose the trust of my family and my team. Between Winn's example and the skills I've gained from hours of time management training through Paul Mitchell Schools, I've adopted some techniques that I would love to share.

Each month I fill out my time management block.

Here's what I do:

1. At the beginning of each month I fill out my time management block for the entire month (sometimes 3 months at a time). I start with all of my "big rocks" (meaning scheduled meetings, seminars, birthdays, events, etc.). I use Google calendar as shown in the illustration below.

Each week I fill out my T's Desk calendar.

---

2. At the beginning of each week I fill out my T's Desk calendar, using the form shown below. This is where I enter specific action items, such as phone calls to make, personal notes to write, things to do, and things to delegate (grouped by urgency and importance) for the entire week.

Each day I go through my
time management block.

3. At the beginning of each day I go through my time management block with
a fine-toothed comb, making sure I've included all of my meetings, my have
to do's, who I'm going to create magic for that day (usually by writing a love
note or taking someone to coffee or lunch), and what I will do in my personal
development time (meaning what I need to study or read that day)

At the end of each day
I evaluate my day.

4. At the end of each day I evaluate my day. This is so important because experience is not the best teacher, evaluated experience is! I ask myself:

- How did my planning go?
- Did I overcommit?
- Did I forget something?
- What did I learn today?
- What did I inspect today? Were there any discoveries?
- What mistakes did I make today?
- How did I hold myself accountable? (Did I follow through with my non-negotiables, such as working out, eating healthy, or following through with things I don't like to do?)
- Who did I hold accountable? (What crucial conversations did I have, or who did I coach or hold accountable that day, and how did I do?)

Talk about being intentional about your day! Most days, I get up at 5 a.m. and usually go to bed by 10 p.m. Some days are so packed and exhausting that some nights, especially in the winter, I'm in bed by 8 p.m.

But I love knowing that I packed my suitcase full and chose my focus well.

FIND WHAT WORKS FOR YOU

Fitness guru Chalene Johnson, another one of my mentors, taught me about another valuable tool. She taught me how to use a reminder app on my smartphone to manage my day and even my thoughts. What we focus on will grow! I use my reminder app to track two key areas:

• **Power Thoughts** – Constant reminders that pop up on my phone throughout the day. These verses help me manage my focus.

• **Reminders** – The app reminds me to put tasks from my balance wheel, job descriptions, tasks for home, etc., into my yearly, weekly, and daily schedules.

When it comes to time management, here's the bottom line: you need to find out what works for you, and **stick to it!** I wasn't always this way, but now that I know what works for me, I am very intentional about scheduling my days.

"Nothing else distinguishes executives as much as their tender loving care of time." – Peter Drucker

WHY TIME MANAGEMENT MATTERS

"When I have the time."

Have you ever had a day that was just *blah* and you couldn't figure out why? Consider that those *blahs* might have come from a broken promise to yourself or someone else.

My time management helps me value others: it helps me prioritize and put others first instead of fitting them in "when I have the time."

In the past few years I've challenged all of my key leaders to become experts in time management, and they have done it! Now I challenge you to do the same. Become an expert in time management.

Be careful not to overcommit, and always over deliver.

You'll find, like I have, that you have fewer of those *blah* days.

DO WHATEVER IT TAKES

In 2012, I joined the John Maxwell Team to train and grow in the areas of leadership, coaching, and speaking. Being part of this elite group has forever changed my life. It has not only transformed me personally and as a business owner, but it has also transformed my relationships with my husband and kids.

If you want to succeed in your quest to Be Amazing, you have to do whatever it takes, too.

Get up early. Stay up later. Give up part of your lunch hour. Put in extra time on the weekends.

EXERCISE:

A STICKY NOTE CAN CHANGE YOUR LIFE

Here's another fun focus finder, done with a simple sticky note.

I do this exercise at least once a year. Try it! You'll be amazed to discover that what you write down actually gets done.

1. Grab a sticky note.

2. In the center, write the word GOALS.

3. Draw up to five branches from the word GOALS.

4. Write up to five goals for the next year.

5. Now fold it up and put it in your wallet or purse.

6. Look at it every time you stand in line, wait at a doctor's office, or any time you're bored.

You'll be amazed to see how quickly you reach your goals.
You move toward what you focus on!

YOUR THOUGHTS BECOME YOUR DESTINY

What are you reading?

Years ago, I read the book *Think and Grow Rich* by Napoleon Hill. At that time, it meant nothing to me, but years later I read it again and got so much out of it. I've read it three times and used it to facilitate mastermind groups (similar to a book study). This is one book I will refer to again and again because every time I read it, I get something new out of it.

What are you reading?

Remember, what you focus on will grow.

I highly recommend *Think and Grow Rich* and any other books that will keep you focused on your goals.

END OF CHAPTER EXERCISE:

BE AMAZING:
CHOOSE YOUR FOCUS

Journaling is a great way to see your thoughts.

For the next 24 hours, jot down notes about your thoughts, both negative and positive.

_____
_____
_____
_____
_____
_____
_____
_____
_____
_____
_____
_____
_____
_____
_____
_____
_____
_____
_____

Take a good look at what you wrote. How much time did you spend on negative thoughts?

If it's time for a change, ask the people around you to hold you accountable to not being negative. At first, they may look at you and ask what you've been "smoking," but trust me, you and they will be better off in the long run.

Your thoughts become words. Your words become actions. Your actions become habits. Your habits become your character. Your character becomes your destiny.

4

CHANGE THE CHANNEL

Are you ready to change the channel in your life?

WHEN I PLAYED high school basketball, even when we won or when I was the high scorer (which happened in most games), I focused on everything I did wrong and beat myself up for it. I carried that thought process into my adult life and realized as a business owner of 17 years that beating myself up had not served me well.

If you want to change your life, or live the life of your dreams, you have to *change the channel*, meaning:

You have to stop doing the things that don't work and spend more time doing the things that lead you toward your goals.

I changed my channel a long time ago. For example, I realized that violent, scary movies never make me feel good about myself, so I don't watch them. How about you? Are you ready to change the channel in your life?

DO THE MATH

In his book *Be Nice (Or Else!)*, Winn Claybaugh offers a great exercise for figuring out how much time we spend on "negative programming" and how much time it takes to erase.

Grab a pencil and do the math!

Calculate how many hours a week you spend each week on negative programming:

Reading the newspaper or online headlines

    _____

Watching the news on television

    _____

Watching soap operas, negative reality shows,
or negative talk shows that degrade others

    _____

Watching movies with negative or violent themes

    _____

Engaging in drama on social media or engaging in gossip
or negative conversations with others

    _____

Total Hours   _____

Multiply by 100   _____

Winn says that for each hour you spend focusing on negative programming or garbage, it takes at least 100 hours of positive programming to counteract the effects. In other words, if you watch a negative, violent movie for two hours, it will take **200 hours** of positive programming to undo the ill effects. Now, there's a reason to change the channel!

STOP REPLAYING OLD MEMORIES

Do you have a Goliath in your life – a big challenge?

To change the channel, you need to stop replaying negative memories and monitor your thought process. You need to be disciplined about what you think about and train your mind to dwell on what's good, positive, and right in your life.

Have you ever noticed that in some families, one family member focuses on the positive but others can't seem to let go of the past? Maybe a lot of unfair things happened to you, but you don't have to dwell on them.

Bitterness imprisons life; love releases it.

Remember, if it's a negative thought it's *not* from God. There is not one place in the Bible that tells us to remember our past hurts or failures. God wants us to focus on what is true, noble, right, pure, lovely, admirable, excellent, or praiseworthy (see Philippians 4:8). He wants us to recall all the miracles and remember the good, not the bad. God gives us beauty for ashes (Isaiah 61:3).

We all have a choice. I could spend my adult life reliving the hurt I had as a teenager, dwelling on my constant struggles, and contemplating suicide, or I could remember the miracles, the wonderful family that loves me, and the friends in my inner circle who believe in me.

What about you? Maybe you're up against this right now. Do you have a Goliath in your life— a big challenge? If you remember the Bible story, Goliath was a big challenge for David but with God's help David beat the challenge. Remember the victories in your life. God can and will raise you higher if you let him.

In business, I've had quite a few Goliaths in my life, including thefts, walkouts, lawsuits, deaths, and personal attacks, to name just a few. When I hire people they become like family to me. If they leave my company, it's like a death. Imagine investing all of your time and energy in someone, and then they vanish from your life. I think that hurts every boss and leader; after all, we're all human.

Despite the pain, I can honestly say those losses made me a better, stronger leader ready to tackle the next challenge—but only because I've trained my mind to think higher thoughts.

I don't dwell on past hurts or pain.

I stopped replaying the painful memories and changed the channel in my mind from the "offended" channel to the "forgiveness" channel. I choose to live a lifestyle of forgiveness. How about you? Which channel do you need to tune into?

A BITTER ROOT PRODUCES BITTER FRUIT

Bitter or better?

Not long ago I presented my motivational speech at a school in New York. During the break, a student shared her bone-chilling story with me. At age 6 months, she had been placed in foster care. Eventually her parents lost their parental rights and she continued in the foster system for years, suffering extreme child abuse, and was finally adopted as a teenager. To say the least, life was often difficult for her and could have easily ruined her.

When I met this young woman, she had a "bitter root"—you could see it in her face—and she didn't know what to do. I looked her straight in the eyes and said,

> "The way I see it, you have two choices: bitter or better."

I didn't say those words to minimize her experience but to encourage her to get rid of her bitter root—to change the channel and stop letting her past hurts destroy her life.

This young woman had not been handed a simple life, and she had a choice to make. She chose better over bitter. With hope, great mentors, and meeting God along the way, she became a success. She graduated from a Paul Mitchell School and became a mentor.

What's important is not her story of horrid abuse, but rather the story of how she chose to overcome her circumstances. Because she changed the channel, she now shows other children in non-ideal situations that, yes, there is hope. If she can make it, so can they. They just have to choose better over bitter.

FORGIVENESS IS THE KEY TO BEING FREE: BE QUICK TO FORGIVE

Since the moment I contemplated suicide and found my value in God, I have always been quick to forgive. After all, God is quick to forgive me of my wrongdoings; how could I not be quick to forgive others in my life?

I never hold grudges, not even against the bullies who called me names as a child and labeled me ugly. I forgave them. I let it go. I had to. And guess what I know now? They were only acting out of their own pain and hurts. Mostly, hurt people hurt people.

Occasionally, being quick to forgive gets me into trouble with my staff. Sometimes I'll want to hire someone back after they've done something wrong. My staff pretty much fired me from hiring because of that, but honestly, I wouldn't change it for the world. I love that about myself!

How about you? Is there someone in your life you need to forgive?

Is there someone or even many people who have wronged you? Forgiveness is the key to being free.

STOP LOOKING IN THE REARVIEW MIRROR

You won't get very far in your car if you're always looking in the rearview mirror. Yes, you need to glance at it once in a while to see if there's anything coming up behind you that could cause an accident, but it's far more important to look out the windshield at the beauty ahead and the opportunities waiting for you.

My husband learned this important lesson in 1995. Here's his story, in his own words, of how he stopped looking in the rearview mirror and chose to focus on the positive aspects of his life.

In August 1995, I had two young children, ages two and three, when my father passed away. All my life I had prayed for his affection, and now he was gone. In that moment, I lost more than a dad; he had also been my law partner for nearly 10 years.

My father had a personality of always wanting to do big, exciting things, like host big parties at his home and take ski trips out west. He had four wives and countless friends, and even his enemies (such as other lawyers) loved him. The local newspaper called him a great litigator and the son of a Supreme Court Justice, yet on his fourth marriage he was no longer nice to his children. The fun times had turned to greed and control and he'd even lied about his incurable cancer so he could drain our law business of all profits. He had majority ownership and control of the business, so he took whatever money he needed, to the detriment of my brother and me, who both had young families to support. He turned his sickness into a pity party that left deep scars to this day.

When my father died, the business was underwater by $100,000. He had turned both judges and attorneys against my brother and me, and he'd written us out of his will entirely so all we had left from his estate was the huge debt. Days before his passing, he had disowned me in a heated, one-sided, berating phone call that caused me to cry like a baby... and that day has never left me.

Yet it's funny how the Holy Spirit lifted me up and carried me when I thought the world had crashed down on me. I was comforted by the ideas that I would succeed in my law practice and that I had a young family who adored me. My children provided the affection I longed for from my dad; they constantly fought for my attention and climbed on me like a big, strong tree. I felt like a kid on a playground!

To bring the business around, I began calling people to tell them we were broke and needed clients. The clients started pouring in, and I was out of debt in six months, thanks to the good Lord and humility on my brother's part. Those were the greatest days I ever had with my brother.

Through this difficult journey, I was also comforted by my beautiful wife Tina, who always gave me hope, encouragement, and lots of prayer. She is the proverbial wind that fills the wings of a wounded eagle and lifts him high.

It was time!

The other angel in my life was my mother, who loved my dad until the day he died. Even though he shattered her world when he divorced her for another woman, my mom was never bitter toward him. Although she was strong, I saw and felt her sadness. She told me to take from my dad all the good memories of life. She always made us kids her priority and it was my turn to do the same. Day by day the steps got wider, and now I only reflect on the good days I had with my dad. Yes, we all have obstacles in our past, but as Winn Claybaugh says in *Be Nice (Or Else!)*, "Let it go. Who cares? Build a bridge and get over it!"

Here's one more example of choosing better over bitter. This one comes from Shaun Chiodo, the young man you met earlier in this book:

I was bitter and angry for so long; I lived in the rearview mirror, never looking forward. It was time for me to change the channel, start forgiving those who had hurt me, and look for the good in everyone. It was time for me to process my thoughts and not lash out. It was time! I set goals and didn't let anything stop me. That's when I decided that I want to be a school owner one day, just like Tina, and help change the lives of everyone around me.

YOUR TONGUE CAN BE YOUR WORST ENEMY

You can tame a tiger but you can't tame a tongue.

The Bible says you can tame a tiger but you can't tame a tongue; it's never been done. "The tongue runs wild, a wanton killer" (James 3:7–10). In case you're wondering, "wanton" is not one of those fortune cookies in a Chinese restaurant. It means "hard to control, undisciplined, unruly."

Not only do you need to monitor your thoughts, you need to monitor your tongue!

I constantly struggle with this area. In the marriage Bible study that my husband and I lead, we recently studied the book of James, which says to "bridle your tongue." I keep praying to God for help with this one, and I constantly have to ask my husband and others to forgive me for my harsh words.

In *Self Improvement 101*, John Maxwell includes the following prayer. A few months before his 60th birthday, he memorized it so he could pray it in the presence of his family and friends on that special day. I've added it to the back of my journal, I pray it often, and like John, I also want to memorize it:

Lord, as I grow older, I think I want to be known as…
Thoughtful, rather than gifted,
Loving, versus quick or bright,
Gentle, over being powerful,
A listener, more than a great communicator,
Available, rather than a hard worker,
Sacrificial, instead of successful,
Reliable, not famous,
Content, more than driven,
Self-controlled, rather than exciting,
Generous, instead of rich, and
Compassionate, more than competent,
I want to be a foot-washer.

No more excuses! Change the channel!

WITH CRISIS COMES OPPORTUNITY

Anything simple will help.

"With crisis comes opportunity" is one of the best leadership lessons I've learned since becoming a John Maxwell coach and speaker. One person who exemplifies that lesson is my friend April, who has learned to praise God through every storm and recognize the opportunities hidden within troubling situations. She has given her problems over to Jesus and knows that, no matter the outcome, she'll be okay. Through every storm, God has changed her into something better, something more beautiful. He is shaping her to fulfill her purpose in the world.

Diagnosed with breast cancer in her 20s, April was considered in remission in 2002. Then in November 2013, what started as seizures turned into a lengthy hospital stay where doctors discovered that her breast cancer had returned with a vengeance. She had two young sons and a third in high school.

Breast cancer was not the only significant challenge April had to overcome. In her late teens and early 20s, she was a victim of domestic abuse. Her boyfriend was verbally and physically abusive and controlling. She had the courage to leave that relationship.

With her second bout of cancer, April underwent aggressive chemotherapy and surgeries. One of the surgeries led to a near septic infection; it was caught just in time and she feels grateful to be alive. Through this, she had the opportunity to experience extreme love and gain awareness of human interactions.

Don't wait for a crisis to give you an opportunity.

April also learned to be obedient when God has a message for her to give. Before one of her surgeries, while praying in the operating room with the doctors and nurses, she saw 20 angels in the room, including three above the surgeon. When she woke up after the surgery, she knew she had to get a message to the surgeon.

The surgeon was no longer available, but April was persistent and made sure she received the message. Shortly after, April received a tearful call from the surgeon thanking her for the message. It was something she needed to hear and April was obedient to God by passing it on.

Recently I took April to a chemo appointment where she brought care packages to lift others up. April knows how to Be Amazing, even in a crisis.

Don't wait for a crisis to give you an opportunity. We can all take time out of our day to make a difference in someone's life. Something as simple as a call, a small care package, or a handwritten letter can make all the difference in the world to someone in pain. Sometimes the right words don't come in difficult situations. Don't use that as an excuse to ignore the hurting person. You don't need the right words—you can just be there for the person. Bring them a meal or even a peanut butter and jelly sandwich, or send them a text to say you're thinking of them and you love them. Anything simple will help. God uses us in all circumstances.
God has a plan for you.

Your job is to Be Amazing in your circumstances.

NO MORE EXCUSES!

What excuses do you keep repeating to not reach your goals?

What excuses do you keep repeating to not reach your goals? Go ahead, write them down. Now cross them out and write "No More Excuses." See below for examples.

I can't do it
I have bad genes
I'm too tired
I've failed before
I'm all done
I hate working out
No willpower
I'll do it later
I'm too old
It's too hard
I'm too busy
I love food

If you keep making excuses, hire a coach or at least find an accountability partner. As my book coach Gail Fink told me recently, "You need someone in your life who won't believe your excuses. Find a coach or accountability partner who can cut right through them."

No More Excuses!

END OF CHAPTER EXERCISE:

BE AMAZING:
CHANGE THE CHANNEL

Take a few minutes to think about the questions below. Jot down the answers and reflect on them every day this week.

1. When it comes to your world, what excuses or blame are you putting on people around you?
_____
_____
_____
_____

2. What will it take for you to accept full responsibility for the results you're getting in your life?
_____
_____
_____
_____

3. What do you need to stop doing?
_____
_____
_____
_____

4. What do you need to start doing?
_____
_____
_____
_____

Are you ready for your life to change? Results . . . they're waiting for you!

5

EXAMINE YOUR HEART

What do you want your legacy to be?

NOT LONG AGO, I attended a funeral. The eulogy for the departed man was absolutely beautiful. People loved him. That was his legacy.

What do you want your legacy to be? That you were unforgiving, a whiner, selfish, an energy vampire? Or do you want people to say you were forgiving, selfless, energetic, and had integrity?

I hope you can hear my heart right now, because my goal is to help you realize that God has destined you to live a victorious life—right now, wherever you are. Some of the most victorious moments in my life happened when I didn't have a lot, like when my husband and I could only afford the salad bar at a local superstore for dinner. We often went there on dates and had the best time together, laughing, carrying on, and enjoying the moment.

God loves you too much for you to live in mediocrity, so what are you waiting for?

Are you waiting for your circumstances to get better? "I'll be happy when ..."? Are you waiting to get more money? Waiting for your ship to come in? Let me ask you this, as my mentor Winn Claybaugh always says: How many ships have you sent out lately?

God wants you to live a victorious life, but you have to make it happen.

WHO ARE YOU AND WHAT DO YOU WANT? GO GET IT!

Author and motivational speaker Erick Thomas (ET) says,

"If you want success as bad as you want to breathe then you'll be successful."

Does your passion get you up in the morning and help you to stay up late, or wake you up in the middle of the night to write down some notes? If the answer is no, then you're living in mediocrity.

You *can* have whatever you want … but you have to know what that is before you can go get it. If you don't know what you want or who you're supposed to be, stop right here.

You have some figuring out to do.

EXERCISE:
WHAT DO YOU WANT?

What would you attempt to do if you knew you couldn't fail?

Take a few minutes and write it in the spaces below.

_____
_____
_____
_____
_____
_____
_____
_____
_____
_____
_____
_____
_____
_____
_____
_____
_____

Take a good look inside your own heart.
If you could describe yourself in ONE word, what would it be?

"If it's to be, it's up to me."

A guest speaker at one of my schools once said, "If you've got an issue with someone ... ISSUE. Get it? It's YOU!" This resonated so much with me. As a leader in Paul Mitchell Schools, I've always learned, "If it's to be, it's up to me." If your life isn't working out the way you want it to, it might be time to quit complaining about everyone around you and see if there are any motives you need to change. You're worth it.

I've heard it said that the two greatest days of our lives are when we are born and when we find out why.

If you're not sure about your purpose in life, you may want to hire a coach to help you figure it out. After all, you'd hire a personal trainer, a therapist, or someone to teach you your favorite hobby. You buy clothes, you buy movies. Why not invest in yourself and figure out what you want? And once you figure it out, don't back down! Give it all you've got! Stop being that fence sitter or resister—that's *not you!* What got you here doesn't matter, just go out and get the life you really want!

WHAT ARE YOU WAITING FOR?

What would I do?

Years ago one of my students came to tell me she had to quit school because she had a disease that affected her muscles and joints and she didn't have long to live. Her doctors told her to go home and get her affairs in order. When she left my office that day, my life was never the same. For the first time in my life I thought, *What if I was facing a terminal disease? Worse yet, what if the doctor told me I had a month to live? What would I do?*

That night, as I researched the Web on life and death, I stumbled upon a website called One Month to Live (www.onemonthtolive.com). I also purchased the book by the same title. The authors challenge readers to live the next 30 days as if they will be your last. At the end of the exercise, I felt more alive than I've ever felt. Based on what I learned, I always ask my audiences to do the following activity, and I encourage you to try it, too.

EXERCISE:

WHAT WOULD YOU CHANGE?

Grab a sticky note.

If you were told you had one month to live, what five things would you change about yourself? Go ahead and write them down. You won't share this with anyone. This is just for you to see.

1.

2.

3.

4.

5.

Now fold the sticky note in half and write on the back, "What am I waiting for?" Put the note in your wallet and look at it often.

YOU CAN'T IGNORE YOUR VALUES

To live a fulfilling life, or a life with purpose, you can't ignore your values. I honestly believe that God gives us our values, and to fall short of them leaves us feeling depressed, lonely, and unfulfilled.

Your values are who you are.

They're at the heart of you. At the end of your life, having lived out your values will help you hear the words, "Well done, good and faithful servant."

Remember the values exercise in chapter 2? Take a few minutes to do it again, as you reflect on the real you, deep in your heart.

EXERCISE:
UNDERSTAND YOUR VALUE

Answer the following questions:

Think of someone who knows you well; someone you'd go to for advice. If they had to describe what you stand for, what would they say? List five values.

1.
2.
3.
4.
5.

Now write five values that are non-negotiable in your life. Don't think too hard on this.

1.
2.
3
4.
5.

Where do these non-negotiable values show up in your day-to-day life?

Which one of these values do you tend to sell out on the most?

You can't do this exercise too often. In fact, I recommend that you look it over every day for the next two weeks, and then do it again four times a year, at the beginning of each season. Last fall my answers were different than this spring. God will show up when you least expect it, a little nudge here, a little nudge there.

THE GIFT OF FORGIVENESS

How about you?

I value my relationship with my husband of more than 27 years and yet I've sold out or neglected that value numerous times. Now, the minute I realize it, I ask for forgiveness. Not long ago my daughter Brianna reminded me that I wasn't appreciating her dad. Once she pointed it out, I asked my husband to write down some things I could do to show him how much I value him. Wow! A heavy load lifted off my heart—just like that. Forgiveness; it's a huge gift.

How about you? Do you have someone you've wronged, or a relationship that went wrong? Go to that person and ask what you can do to show you value your relationship.

If you're not sure what to say, Winn Claybaugh teaches a wonderful little script: "I was wrong. Forgive me. Can we please start over? Can you tell me three things I can do to show you how much I value our relationship?"

Stop reading this book right now. Visit or call the person you're thinking of and ask those questions. Then come back to this book and write down the three actions you can take to show how much you value him or her.

1.
2.
3.

Now meditate on these things.
Be intentional about them and follow through.

TRANSFORMATIONAL LEADERSHIP: YOU CAN'T GIVE WHAT YOU DON'T HAVE

On my John Maxwell Team journey, I've learned that the highest form of leadership is leading ourselves. Maxwell says, "Everything rises and falls on leadership," and that hit me hard when it truly sank in. The idea that "you can't give what you don't have" has been so big for me; I had it wrong my entire life. I had spent almost 20 years as a business owner trying to fix and change people around me when I should have looked in the mirror to fix and change myself. It took me a few weeks, if not months, to realize that my employees were not responsible for the results I was getting; that was and continues to be my responsibility.

Maxwell calls this *transformational leadership:* when you start by transforming yourself, you transform people around you. Or, as Winn Claybaugh says,

"If it's to be, it's up to me."

Take your finger and point it at someone. How many fingers point back at you? That's right—three! What a great little reminder to spend three times as much time on yourself as you spend trying to fix and change other people.

This concept truly sank in when I had the opportunity to travel with 150 other John Maxwell Team coaches to train leaders in Guatemala. We spent three days being trained, then three days training 24,000 Guatemalan leaders on how to conduct round tables (a system of examining our hearts, applying values and laws to our lives, and taking action). Inadvertently, I was the one who got trained, and I will never be the same. A year and a half later I'm definitely not where I want to be, but I'm also far from where I was.

Will you take a risk?

As soon as I got home, I began teaching the system to a core group of staff, students, and key leaders in Paul Mitchell Schools so we could teach all 16,000 future professionals and staff. Talk about taking risks! Even though I'm afraid of failure, I will move forward with courage because I know God has called me to teach this to my circle of influence.

Do you want to wake up one day and find that you're 95 years old and filled with regret for not taking risks? When you begin to make yourself your responsibility, growth happens. All it took for me to learn this valuable lesson was to let go of my ego and be vulnerable and transparent.

Will you take a risk?
Will you examine your heart?

WHAT KIND OF LEADER ARE YOU?

Shaun Chiodo did the exercise at the end of this chapter, on his path to success:

I am glad to say that examining my heart today you will see so much love and care for the people in my life. I am not a complainer about things; I accept the things I cannot change and change the things I can.

Life is about perspective, and I had a very warped version of what life was for a very long time. I felt alone and depressed every day and I turned to people who were not my friends but who saw my success and wanted to bring me to their level.

I was angry when one of my best friends died in a car crash, I was angry that my parents got divorced, I was angry my dad was never there and lied all the time, I was angry that my family had to go through a lot of court time because of molestation, I was angry that I was coming out and not feeling accepted, I was angry that AIDS killed another one my friends, I was angry that my relationships were always physically and verbally abusive.

I did not know what love was; why would I? I had never seen it until I came into such a positive world, started to examine my heart, and realized that I am loved by those around me and I need to get back on track!

Are you ready to find out what kind of leader you are and where you need to transform yourself? Then try this exercise, excerpted from John Maxwell's *The 21 Irrefutable Laws of Leadership Workbook*.

END OF CHAPTER EXERCISE:
BE AMAZING:
EXAMINE YOUR HEART

The Law of Respect: Having the People Who Know Me the Best Respect Me the Most

This week gather three of your friends for a discussion. Come up with five situations that you and your friends might find yourself in as a group (e.g., planning a vacation, opening a business together, playing a sport, planning an event). For each situation, have each person tell which person in the group they would most likely follow and why.

Situation 1
Leader _____ Why _____

Situation 2
Leader _____ Why _____

Situation 3
Leader _____ Why _____

Situation 4
Leader _____ Why _____

Situation 5
Leader _____ Why _____

Who was named the leader the most times?
Leader _____ Why? _____

Who was named the leader the fewest times?
Leader _____ Why? _____

How often were you named the leader? _____
How can you gain more respect? _____

6

SOW AND GROW

"Help others get what they want, and you'll get what you want."

BY THIS TIME NEXT YEAR, as I continue with the John Maxwell Team training, I will not be the same person as I am today. Two lessons that truly changed my life came from John Maxwell himself, who says his purpose is to "add value to others" and whose signature statement is "Help others get what they want, and you'll get what you want." In other words, if you sow an extraordinary seed, you will reap an extraordinary harvest.

There it is: You sow and you grow!

If I continue to sow, I'll continue to grow into a new and improved version of myself. There's no doubt in my mind.

"Giving is the highest level of living."
– John Maxwell

LIVING A LIFESTYLE
OF GENEROSITY

"Success unshared is failure."

Through the years I've met quite a few people, including my wonderful business partners, who have taught me to live a lifestyle of generosity. This section includes several examples of extremely successful mentors who sowed into the lives of others and grew beyond their wildest dreams.

My business partner and mentor **John Paul DeJoria**'s philosophy is "Success Unshared Is Failure," and the Paul Mitchell company's slogan is "Giving Back Is the New Black." I honestly believe John Paul is one of the world's richest men because of the sowing he's done in the lives of others.

He tells an amazing life-changing story about the first time he had a few extra dollars in his pocket, after finally taking the Paul Mitchell company "out of the red." He went into a restaurant and noticed two women and several children getting ready to eat. Having been down on his luck for many years, John Paul recognized the same signs in this group and decided to secretly pay their bill. When one of the women realized what had happened, she yelled out to everyone in the restaurant, "Whoever you are, BLESS you!"

I honestly believe John Paul is one of the world's richest men because of the sowing he's done in the lives of others.

"Life is all about shifts and vision."

Winn Claybaugh, my business partner and the author of *Be Nice (Or Else!)*, is a selfless example of a sower. Over the years, he has poured his life into thousands and thousands of future professionals (students) in our Paul Mitchell Schools and taught us all how to give back. To date, Paul Mitchell Schools have raised and donated over $15.2 million to national and local nonprofit organizations because of Winn's leadership and the efforts of our Paul Mitchell future professionals and staff. Giving back is part of our curriculum: we teach the value of "when you sow, you grow" in our Paul Mitchell Schools.

Another one of my mentors, **David Wagner**, wrote a book called *Life as a Daymaker: How to Change the World by Making Someone's Day.* David's book includes several stories about how he sowed into people's lives as a hairdresser. In one especially life-changing story, a woman came into David's salon to have her hair done. David had no idea that she planned to commit suicide that night and wanted her hair to look good for her funeral. The way he poured into her life that night gave her new hope to live. Instead of taking her life, she went home to get help for her depression. Daymaker!

John Maxwell Team president **Paul Martinelli** teaches a class called "The 7 Levels of Awareness," a concept that I often teach in my leadership and mastermind classes around the country. If you're feeling frustrated or stuck in your life, Paul recommends that you commit to tithing 10 percent and watch what happens. "I don't know how it happens," he says, "it just does." I've made it a point in my personal life to set up a giving plan instead of an income plan, and I can tell you, it works!

BLOOM WHERE YOU'RE PLANTED

The "sow and grow" philosophy has also helped **Shaun Chiodo**. Shaun says:

Because I have given back to the school and the person who changed my life, I have reaped extraordinary rewards. I became a daymaker and a person of excellence and I am living to give every day.

Life is all about shifts and vision. I started envisioning my success and my future when I met Tina Black five years ago, and my life changed. I am a happy, successful person with no regrets in life because I know that everything I've been through has made me who I am. I am truly thankful for having sat through Tina's success class. It changed my life and actually saved my life.

Sowing and growing means you need to bloom where you're planted. No matter what you've been dealt in life—whether you feel like you're in a barren wasteland or the lushest garden—you need to be the best that you can be.

If you don't bloom where you're planted and instead spend your time being negative and complaining about your situation, you will never be blessed with more. Suppose you bought your kids a bike and they whined, moaned, and complained about it. Would you really want to give them a newer bike? Heck no! You'd probably rather give them a spanking or a time out. Or suppose you had a job at McDonald's and you spent all your time complaining about your boss and the hours you worked. I don't think your manager would promote you, and I don't think God would, either.

Are you blooming where you're planted?

I've been grateful for almost every job I've ever had in my entire life, and I bloomed where I was planted. At almost every job, I was the number-one employee, I made the most money, and every boss loved me. I always had an owner's mentality.

You'll notice that I said "almost" every job. I'm terribly embarrassed to admit that I was not a good employee at two of my jobs. At one of them, all I did was complain about my boss and everything he did wrong. I was in a "holding pattern" at that time: I held my own growth back. At the second job, when I was 19 years old, a customer neglected to give me a tip, so I wrote in the 15% tip for myself. I was immediately fired from that job. To this day, I still feel sick about it.

I learned from that mistake and became the most honest employee anyone ever had. In my last job before I became an entrepreneur (20 years ago), I worked hours that I was never paid for, I wrote articles for free to promote the business, and I honestly treated the company as if it was my own. Five years later, *boom*, I bought my own business. I honestly believe that if I had not bloomed where I was planted for those five years, owning my own company never would have happened.

How about you? Are you blooming where you're planted? Are you the number-one employee? Why not? What's holding you back?

THE JOY OF GIVING

It's better to give than receive.

Trust me: when you sow, you grow!

If you're not satisfied with where you are in every step of your life, you won't be granted more. I've listened to people whine, moan, and complain throughout their entire lives, only to continue to whine, moan, and complain some more. When you choose a lifestyle of gratitude, growth just happens.

Giving has always come easily to me; my parents taught me the joy of giving throughout my entire life. My dad always told us it's better to give than to receive, and it's so true. I've received so many amazing gifts over the years but nothing surpasses the joy of giving to someone who can't repay you.

Giving truly is the highest level of living.

EXERCISE:
WHAT CAN YOU DO?

Try this activity to help you
practice sowing and growing.

Think about a time in the past week, month, or year when someone sowed into your life. Write it down.

How did it make you feel?

Now think of a time in the past week, month, or year when YOU sowed into someone's life and write it down.

How did that make you feel?

What can you do in this next week to sow into someone else's life?

ORGANIZATIONS THAT SOW AND GROW

Sadly, many in our American society have isolated themselves in the pursuit of "success" and found themselves detached from family and friends. They've lost the element of sowing into others' lives. Fortunately, many individuals and organizations take the initiative to sow the seeds of kindness.

One of my jobs in the Paul Mitchell Schools is to lead the nationwide network of Be Nice (Or Else!) teams. My school director, Shaun Chiodo, leads our nationwide Be Nice Team webinars, which feature incredible leaders like David Wagner, Winn Claybaugh, and John Paul DeJoria, just to name a few, talking about why they think being nice is a prerequisite for success. You sow and you grow.

Paul Mitchell Schools also participate in a yearly Free Hugs Day, where students and staff members go out to hug random people. We've hugged everyone from homeless and elderly individuals to top business executives. Many of these people break down and cry, telling us that they'd just lost a loved one and needed our hug, or they hadn't been hugged in years.

Are you part of a "sow and grow" community? Would you like to start one?

END OF CHAPTER EXERCISE:
BE AMAZING: SOW AND GROW

Here are some of my favorite resources for gathering ideas on how to sow and grow. Take a few minutes right now to research these organizations (or others that you love) and come up with five ways that you can give back in the next week, month, and year.

- Random Acts of Kindness: www.randomactsofkindness.org
- David Wagner's Daymaker website: www.daymaker.net
- *Be Nice (Or Else!)* by Winn Claybaugh: available at www.beniceorelse.com
- *Intentional Living* by John Maxwell
- John Maxwell's 30 Day Journey: http://bit.ly/1KbK3tM

Next week:

Next month:

Next year:

7

STOP MAKING EXCUSES

"Get off the excuse bus!"

BACK IN 2002 when I heard Winn Claybaugh say, "If you're good at coming up with excuses, you'll never be good at anything else," I wanted to put it on T-shirts, banners, business cards, and billboards. I wanted to post it *everywhere* because it hit me right in the face. Why? Because that's exactly how I was (and still am, on occasion)—the biggest excuse maker in the world.

Flash forward to 2013 when I heard this message from John Maxwell: "Transformation begins in me." Superstar hairstylist and salon owner Kelly Cardenas, another one of my mentors, tells his audiences to stop living in the land of excuses, or Blameville, as he calls it, and "Get off the excuse bus!" Thanks to their wise teaching, I now know that if I don't take 100 percent responsibility for everything that happens to me, I'm acting like a victim and I will never move forward.

LIFE-CHANGING MANTRAS

"There's nothing to worry about ever."

In the last few years since joining the John Maxwell Team, I've developed mantras that have helped rid me of my excuses. (And by the way, I realized that my excuses were just a decoy to protect me from facing my limiting beliefs.)

I used to be a huge, huge worrier. I'll never forget when I was in Guatemala and one of my coaches, Scott Faye, told me, "There's nothing to worry about ever." It hit me like a ton of bricks that day, as if God had sent that message to me through Scott. It became my personal mantra that year. In fact, I taught it to a lot of other worriers, and to this day, I still hear some of them say it. That mantra relieved a ton of stress and gave me much more faith that everything will always work out.

During my second year on the team my mantra became, "With crisis comes opportunity." Talk about perfect timing: boom, I was diagnosed with a precancerous lesion, and I can tell you, that crisis brought me huge opportunities. I became an education ambassador for the nonprofit breast and ovarian cancer awareness organization Bright Pink, where a dream of mine is coming true this year: I've always wanted to speak and teach college students and this year I am teaching over 1,000 college sorority students how to prevent breast and ovarian cancer through Bright Pink.

With crisis comes opportunity!

Do you have a mantra to get rid of your excuse?

Another one of my mantras is "Failure is my friend." This one is huge for me and has given me much more strength. Admitting my faults and weaknesses and growing from my failures has helped me get rid of excuses that were no more than decoys to cover up my own shame.

My newest mantra is "It's my fault." I learned it recently from my mentor Kelly Cardenas, and oh my, can I tell you how much more peace I have? Now when a problem happens at home with my husband or kids, whether I think it's my fault or not I immediately say, "It's my fault," and lo and behold, I feel immediate peace. Yes, peace! Recently I lost two significant staff members and instead of getting upset or gossiping about them I immediately said, "It's my fault," and all of my stress was gone. This statement puts me into instant solution mode and takes me out of excuse and blame mode. Excuses and blame are exhausting! I've had more energy than ever since taking on this mantra.

Do you have a mantra to get rid of your excuses? If not, you can borrow mine. Here they are again:

- There's nothing to worry about ever.
- With crisis comes opportunity.
- Failure is my friend.
- It's my fault.

TAKE 10 PERCENT SHIFTS

Small shifts, small goals.

So how do you take 100 percent responsibility and make big changes in your life? You do it in small, 10 percent shifts. When I heard that advice from Winn Claybaugh and his team years ago, I thought, *Okay, that's not so bad, I can do that.*

Put one foot in front of the other.

Small shifts, small goals.

GET SMART

"Action plans."

Do you know the biggest difference between you and people like John Paul DeJoria, Oprah Winfrey, and Dr. Martin Luther King, Jr.? Brilliant leaders know how to maximize their time. Another one of my mentors, fitness guru Chalene Johnson, who spoke at one of our school owners' summits, taught me something so valuable. She taught me how to use my smart phone so I can maximize my time, too.

Chalene told us to do whatever it took to invest in an easy-to-use smart phone—even if it meant foregoing food, clothing, purses, shoes (you get the picture). Now, close this book and go get a smart phone, if you don't already have one! I personally use the iPhone to maximize my time. I think it's one of those phones for dummies (if I can use it you can, too).

One of my favorite features on my phone is its apps, especially the reminder app on Google calendar. This one automatically comes with my phone. The reminder app has different categories, including my to-do list. When I'm standing in a long line at the grocery store, or sitting on an airplane, I review my "Power Thoughts" category, which includes Bible verses I want to memorize and things I'm working on in my life. Another one of my categories is "Action Plans." These are the plans I have set to focus on each week after I meet with my team or have a roundtable with the groups I facilitate. I also have a category named "21 Indispensable Qualities of a Leader," taken from John Maxwell's book, so I can read and focus on those characteristics each day.

Chalene taught me that if I checked my reminder app as often as I check my text messages, I'd reach my goals and dreams faster than I ever imagined. In fact, she challenged me to check my reminder app every time before I check my text messages. I challenge you to do that, too.

Grab your smart phone and let's make some categories! Review the lists you made in this book and turn them into categories in your reminder app. Here are a few other suggestions for your categories:

- Five things you'd change if you knew you had a month to live
- Five ways to give back
- Five non-negotiables in your life
- What you'd attempt to do if you knew you wouldn't fail
- Five goals in the next year
- Balance wheel

Get creative!
Put these in your reminder app now.

FAIL TO PLAN OR PLAN TO FAIL

Since I joined the John Maxwell Team, I've discovered the need to be more intentional about my growth. I realized I wasn't including my dreams, goals, and growth focuses in my schedule, so I started to use my new daily schedule forms (you saw them in chapter 3, Choose Your Focus). Here's another example:

How was my planning?

At the beginning of each month, I sit down for an hour and plan out my month. I schedule all of my meetings, put reminders in my reminder apps, and schedule my professional growth strategies (such as my roundtables, masterminds, coaching training, speaking training, seminars, and webinars) and my personal growth strategies (such as listening to motivational CDs by Joel Osteen, MASTERS CDs by Winn Claybaugh, CDs by the Life Business, daily inspirational messages by Christian author and speaker Joyce Meyer, and TED Talks, to name a few). At the end of that hour, I see what percentage of my time is scheduled for personal growth. If it's less than 10 percent, I need to go back to my schedule and start inserting those items.

At the beginning of each week, I plan the week by reviewing my Google calendar, reminder app, and growth strategy.

Every morning around 5 a.m., I pull out my daily schedule and get even more intentional. I look closely at my "have to do's," decide how I will create magic that day, and plan my study time.

At the end of each day, I evaluate my day.

- How was my planning?
- What did I learn?
- What did I discover?
- How did I hold myself accountable?

Can you imagine going on a road trip without any pre-planning?

This strategy truly has been life changing and so much FUN! I use a lot of fun markers and lots of color so I stay engaged. I urge you to try it. Your life will never be the same when you master your time management.

Can you imagine going on a road trip from Michigan to California and getting into the car without any pre-planning? No map, no GPS. Would you get very far very fast? You might make it to your destination eventually, if you stop for directions along the way, but it would take so much longer than if you had planned and ordered your steps. That's how many of us go through life, including me! Sometimes I'll get out of bed and go through my day with no pre-planning or order, just one foot in front of the other. It's SCARY, but I've done that most of my life.

I'm glad I wrote this chapter, because now I'm accountable. In fact, when you see me, ask me if I'm true to my word. Hold me accountable, and I'll hold you accountable, too.

DO IT AFRAID

I'll never forget the day Winn Claybaugh told all of the school owners at one of our organization's first meetings that we needed to become motivational speakers. That was after he told us that people's number one fear is the fear of public speaking, second only to their fear of death by fire!

I remember that day so vividly; I even remember where I was sitting. You know that feeling you get when someone is talking and you think they're looking right at you? That's how I felt—like I was the only person in the room, and he had singled me out. My palms felt like fire; my heart was palpitating. I didn't even like to speak in front of two people at a time, but when Winn said I had to become a motivational speaker, I thought, *Okay, Winn. I'll "do it afraid."*

Talk about taking a risk! Holy smokes!

But today if you asked my staff, they'd tell you I crave the stage, love the microphone, and they can't get me to shut up or get off the stage.

END OF CHAPTER EXERCISE:
BE AMAZING: STOP MAKING EXCUSES

The only way to Be Amazing is to be intentional about your personal growth.

Don't be obsessed with money, success, or whatever external things you think will make you happy. Rather, be obsessed with constantly improving yourself. Transformation begins in YOU!

As we wrap things up, here's your game plan for improvement: Review the 7-step SUCCESS formula, identify a 10 percent shift that you can start making now in each category, and write them down.

Come on, you can do this! It will be FUN! To keep your momentum high, review your list every morning and then say this 50 times: DO IT NOW!

No regrets. Just do it!

Category	My 10% Shifts
Stalk Visionaries	
Understand Your Value	
Choose Your Focus	
Change the Channel	
Examine Your Heart	
Sow and Grow	
Stop Making Excuses	

8

AMAZING STORIES, AMAZING PEOPLE

JUST LIKE YOU!

THINK YOU HAVE IT ROUGH? A STORY FROM POVERTY TO SUCCESS

AT SOME POINT in your life you will face adversity. Everyone does. What's important is how you choose to overcome that adversity. There have been several mentors in my life who have demonstrated how to overcome adversity. I learned from them and you can, too.

One of my strong influencers is my father, who has so many values that are universally good.

My father grew up in a difficult financial situation, without his father around. Dad started working at age 12. At age 15 he quit school and worked in a factory to help his family and his older sister (she was still in school and he wanted to buy her a dress for graduation). He went from nothing to helping a business grow from $3 million to $1.2 billion.

When Dad looks back at what propelled him in his life, he realizes that he wanted to get ahead. He wanted more out of life, and he wanted to support his family in a better way.

Dad recalls some great advice he received: "There was a neighbor who had his own business who I used to talk to. One day he said that I need to just sit down, figure out what I'm going to be doing on day one up through five years from now."

My dad did that. He sat down, took a leap of faith, and said to himself, *In one year I'd like to be here, and I'd like the money to be here,* and so forth. He worked hard and reached his five-year goal in two years. He achieved his next five-year goal in one year and became a huge success at the top of his company.

Dad is an extremely giving person who supported his mom as long as she needed it. He always gave, even when he didn't have abundance. He trusted that he would be okay as long as he was generous. He was raised in a close family and believed that when something goes wrong, you help your family. "When people are hurting, you got to try to help," he'd say.

My dad always taught me to add value for people. As a result, I look for people I can help and I always know it comes back a hundredfold, not only financially, but also in the chance to see how those people's lives change.

My parents' marriage has also been an ideal example for me. All of my dad's siblings were married two, three, or four times yet he has been married to my mom for over 58 years. Dad says the secrets are love and learning from your mistakes.

MORE TIPS FROM DAD: STAY POSITIVE, LISTEN AND LEARN

"Don't make the same mistake twice," he says.

Dad also taught that the biggest thing you can do in life is to do the little things—the things you say you will. If you tell someone you're going to call, call. If you tell someone you'll give them something, give it to them. It's not the big things. Those little things mean so much to people. I always live by them.

When I was growing up my dad always said, "Okay, you guys, you can cry about this for one or two minutes but now put a smile on your face." It always helps you to stay positive.

I asked him how he got past his childhood circumstances without becoming a victim and he said, "It's all on you." He said:

You can sit back and help yourself or you can sit back and have someone help you. I never wanted a handout. I wanted to work for what I got, I wanted to be positive all the time. And sometimes when I wasn't positive, I kicked myself in the ass and moved on. It's so important that you stay positive in life, and I've always done that. Regardless of what you're going through in life—because you know you have to go through a lot of different things—if you keep a smile on your face, you do feel better. And I've found that you normally start feeling that. I kind of keep it very straightforward, happy-like, and it really works out for me.

Little things mean so much.

Dad also taught me that you can learn from others by listening and watching. Successful people listen and learn from other people. I asked my dad how he learned from others and he said:

I watch people. You have to have the capacity to listen, and even if you know the answers you have to listen. If not, sometimes you just stop people from talking and you cut in when you're supposed to be listening. You might know what they're going to say 50 or 80 percent of the time. That leaves at least 20 percent of the time where you are going to learn something. Maybe they see in a different light than you.

On several different occasions, I attended retailer conference presentations with over 5,000 people featuring the Retailer of the Year. I had the opportunity to hear Sam Walton from Walmart, Harry Cunningham from Kmart, and even J. C. Penney speak. All three of them had the same identical message during their speeches—you have to have the capacity to listen. I caught that in all three of them.

Sometimes you don't have the time to listen. If you don't have the time, take the time to say, "Let me get back to you because I want to continue with this conversation." But if you do have the time, stay there and listen to what they have to say. Sometimes it's a complaint. Sometimes it's an interview. While you're listening, make people comfortable around you. To do this, I make light of things. You have to listen.

MOM'S UNCONDITIONAL LOVE

While my dad was a great financial success, my mom Sissy was the backbone who allowed it to happen. She raised five successful kids with unconditional love. She instilled in us the love of God. She is all about God, Jesus, and love.

As if raising five successful kids wasn't enough of a success story, in adulthood my mom had her own success story of overcoming addition. The fact that she became a prescription drug addict is even more shocking when you hear her background.

Mom grew up in a Christian Science family and never took medications or went to a doctor until she was pregnant with her first child at age 21. That sounds like a person who would never have issues with prescription medication, right? Then at age 38 she experienced a huge anxiety problem. One day she went to the bank with one of her young daughters and couldn't even sign her name. She felt so much anxiety that she was helpless at the bank. In that era, Valium was the treatment for many problems, including anxiety. She took it on and off for a while, and none of us realized she had an anxiety issue; she kept it hidden from us kids and my dad. Eventually she stopped taking it, on her own. That wasn't her addiction issue, but it was her introduction to using medication to deal with her issues.

In her early 50s, my mom developed an alcohol dependency that none of the family knew about; we learned later, when she told us. She stopped drinking for about five years, and then she was on and off of alcohol and other drugs prescribed for legitimate medical purposes—Oxycontin, Ambien, and Ativan.

In 2013 she broke her hip and went into the hospital. She came out with Oxycontin. That December, the family realized that Mom wasn't herself—she was too drugged up. Even though she didn't think she needed to detox, we took her to the hospital to get her off the Oxycontin and Ambien.

While she initially fought us, she eventually decided she didn't want disappoint anyone, let alone herself. She didn't want people's last memory of her being that she couldn't do it, and she apologized for her initial anger.

Our whole family is so proud of her. We hadn't seen her look so good in years. We were initially numb to her having problems. One thing that helped us confront her was something she taught us: you have to love someone for who they are and come at them where you can in a loving way. You should never fight and bicker. You need to be there for one another.

Mom taught us that even seniors can have major life issues that they need to overcome. She didn't stay stuck in her pity party. She had ice in her veins and took the challenge to overcome her addiction. Now she wants to help raise awareness about prescription drug addiction and encourage others that they, too, can overcome it.

Now faced with a terminal diagnosis of pulmonary fibrosis, Mom continues with her positive attitude. She says, "You need to live in the moment and spend the time you have because it's up to God when you leave."

My mom and dad have led me down the path of success with their great examples. These great role models have overcome major issues and helped me realize that, at some point in life, we will all face challenges.

LOVE SCAR

My sister-in-law Liz is another amazing woman who made it through adversity. She learned that through God we can Be Amazing.

Liz's parents divorced when she was a child, and her dad's absence left a huge void in her life. She looked to her brother Bryan (my husband) as a father figure.

For a time when she was younger, Liz thought she was clinically depressed. She was drinking and doing other things she shouldn't have. Her grandmother was her saving grace, taking her to church where she learned that Christ loved her. If she hadn't known this, she would have committed suicide.

As a young adult Liz felt that God was talking to her about getting back to church. She found a church and rededicated her life to Christ. At that point she knew wanted a family. She eventually met her husband on a blind date, married him, and had three daughters.

As life progressed, they kept moving in an effort to "keep up with the Joneses." Eventually, they lost their life savings from all the moving. Liz spent less time going to church and studying God's word. Things started getting worse and worse.

Liz now realizes she was not putting God first. Now they put God first and are doing very well. One day a coworker noticed a lump on Liz's neck. A doctor told her it was fine but Liz felt God telling her she was not okay. A second opinion revealed that she had stage 3 thyroid cancer.

Now Liz stays in God's word. She says we have a positive, trusting God and we need to lean on him. She says the only way she made it through this difficult time was trusting in God's will. Liz also says we need to enjoy every moment. She takes what she has and works with it. She chooses to be happy, even in the bad times. It is all about a choice, a daily choice. Liz tries to be humble and walk in God's word.

Now she says the "love scar" on her neck reminds her of her strengths and what God has given her. Do you have a love scar—either internal or external— that reminds you of the strength God has given you?

Life is all about daily choices.

THE LORD IS WITH YOU

Some people face difficult struggles but you'd never know unless you were told. One of those women is my mother-in-law, Virginia Carman. She faced many struggles in her life, including a treacherous divorce from her first husband and the father of their three children. After the divorce, she finished her degree and taught full time. Eventually she remarried.

Unfortunately that marriage was similar to the first, and her second husband passed away after a seven-year battle with Alzheimer's disease.

Throughout her life, Virginia has wanted to be kind to people and be treated that way. She always knows the Lord is with her and will help her overcome. She learned from her adversity and doesn't regret it because it made her a better person.

JOY, SPIRITUALLY CENTERED

Sarah was a typical teenager who faced some not-very-typical teenage circumstances, including the death of her best friend. Two weeks after the devastating news, Sarah found herself still in bed, so other friends grabbed her out of her room to take her up north. While there, she received a shocking call from her brother, who said their dad might be dead and she needed to come home. Later she learned the details: a valve in his heart had exploded.

Ten minutes after the emergency crew arrived, they were driving him to the hospital without their flashing lights, which is what they do when someone has passed away. Suddenly the lights came on. It was a miracle! The doctors called it a Lazarus moment. At the hospital, Sarah's dad was put on life-support machines and the family was told that this would be his life.

Two weeks later, the doctors started talking about taking him off the machines. Of course, Sarah's mom was with him the whole time. Another miracle: he regained consciousness. He had short-term memory issues, but he could remember long term. He eventually became a case study at a medical school.

Watching her dad go through rehabilitation was humbling for Sarah. Visiting him every day and watching him learn to tell time and eat food again forced her to grow up fast. It seemed like every month he was back in the hospital for surgery or complications, but after eight months he made it home. The family was grateful to have him around. He lived a basically normal life, but his struggles with walking, not working, and going through this situation left him with depression.

Several years later, life was good and down to a routine... until Sarah's mom went in for rotator cuff surgery and discovered that she had diabetes and needed open-heart surgery. Her mom's health started to deteriorate.

Most people have the opportunity to care for their parents in their 50s; Sarah had the chance in her 20s. At this point, she was helping her parents with their bills. With her dad unable to work, they moved from a luxurious house to a trailer.

During this time, Sarah started at the Paul Mitchell School. One day she received one of the best calls ever from one of her mentors. She rushed home to tell her dad. When she opened his bedroom door to tell him, he had passed away. He had lived for seven years on borrowed time and was now gone. Not knowing whether his death was God's choice or her dad's choice gave Sarah a lot of uncertainty and vulnerability.

In what became a spiritual journey for her, Sarah gained strength from helping her mom who was legally blind from diabetes. She moved her mom to an apartment for safety and visited every Sunday. For the next year, as Sarah healed from her grief, she knew it was okay not to be okay. Then one Sunday, her mom didn't answer the phone. When Sarah got to her mom's apartment, she found one of the scariest things she had ever seen. Her mom was on the bathroom floor, shaking and having difficulty breathing. Sarah called 911 and kept telling her mom she loved her. She said it over and over again.

Sarah thought, God wouldn't do this to me. God wouldn't let her mom die. She died.

Now Sarah had the deaths of two parents to grieve. She thought she was too young to be going through this, but then she decided to honor them with a legacy. She let their life be proof of their love. Her dad loved to laugh and her mom loved to make people feel special. Sarah carries on this joy.

Sarah found strength by letting herself be weak. She surrounded herself with the right people and mentors. She knew that her thoughts would cultivate her life.

Sarah sees every day as an opportunity to make her parents proud. This brought her to exactly who she is today: a young woman who feels very lucky to have grown up with two incredible parents. She feels there is a reason she went through this and it will be part of how she helps people. We live our life's purpose when we help more than just ourselves.

Since then, three of Sarah's closest friends have lost a parent, and Sarah was able to be a glimmer of light and strength to them.

Looking back, Sarah realized she made a choice. She could have fallen into a victim's role, but she decided instead to put her best foot forward. Her parents still live through her. She also knows that other people have been through so much more.

As one of her mentors, I am amazed at her fast growth. Sarah overcame huge adversity, stayed positive, and chose to put her best foot forward. What an honor to her parents.

ATTITUDE OF GRATITUDE

Another colleague, Shelly Aristizabal, author of *This Is Your Year,* went from a peak to a valley and back to a peak. Sometimes when you're on top and crash down, it can be hard to recover, but Shelly found a way to recover professionally, spiritually, and physically.

Shelly always believed that adversity makes us stronger and prepares us for what's next. Her parents were teenagers when they had her. She was a big dreamer and thought she could make a difference in the world. She was not "grounded in reality" like others who surrounded her.

One of Shelly's memorable moments took place when she was 19 years old, after her grandfather passed away. She spilled her guts to a stranger sitting next to her about the big dreams she had. He encouraged her to read *The Greatest Salesman in the World* by Og Mandino, which taught her the value of perseverance and mentors and the magic of big thinking. She also learned that most successful people want others to succeed, too.

Shelly applied those principles and became a great success in the gold industry. She had four kids and life was good. When her youngest child was two years old, Shelly had a nervous breakdown. She felt bad for wondering why she wanted more out of life.

Then she went to a network-marketing event and within 17 months became one of the top people in the company. She felt like she was stepping into greatness. She was making people healthy and helping others make money. But she got out of balance and focused strictly on business. God had his own way of communicating this to her: he showed her through a crisis and subsequent miracle.

As Shelly was giving a presentation to a group that included doctors, she felt funny. The doctors knew right away what the issue was: a hemorrhage in her brain. Very little can be done for this condition: half of the affected people die from it, and 90 percent of those who survive have brain damage. Shelly was fortunate to be near a hospital renowned for this type of problem, and she miraculously survived with no damage.

That was five years ago. Now every day Shelly wakes up and asks why she is alive. She also asks what she can do to create significance and make a difference. She left the network-marketing business because she didn't think it was the direction she should go. She learned to let go and not try to control all situations. She realized that God has a plan and we need to love others and live life to the fullest. Now Shelly can relate to so many women about balance and pain. She can help and encourage them.

Since these changes, blessings keep pouring into her life. One of these is the opportunity to work with Nancy Fitzgerald from Anchors Away Ministry on an anti-bullying curriculum for high school juniors, seniors, and parents, the number one influence on kids' lives.

Shelly maintains an attitude of gratitude. From her example, we can learn that a positive attitude will get us through obstacles and challenges. If you start every day with a list of three to five things you are truly grateful for and why you are grateful for them, it will truly change your life.

TRAGEDY FOR THE GOOD

My good friend Lisa Price shared the inspiring story of her brother Dan, who died a few years ago after battling amyotrophic lateral sclerosis (ALS), the progressive neurodegenerative condition known as Lou Gehrig's disease. Although he was facing death, Dan still lived his life's purpose. Here's Lisa's story, in her own words.

My brother Dan was the most amazing person I have ever met. He is the reason I became a Christian, why I homeschooled, and why I believe that there are real men and women of God.

He was married with five children, and our families grew up and played together and fought together and laughed together and cried together. When he was diagnosed, he told me first. He told me he was believing and praying and willing to do whatever God's will was. We have a huge family: 12 kids and a whole lot of drama. We had just lost our other brother, Ron, to a drunk driver, and then my nephew died in a tragic rock climbing expedition with his father; he was only 23.

As Danny's disease progressed, he told me he believed the reason he was special enough to be chosen for this was that the Lord wanted to use him as the vessel to bring the family to Jesus. After all the turmoil and angst we had had, we were all searching.

Well, lo and behold, this did happen. Families were saved. This man of God stood before his entire congregation to tell his story. Our parents heard it—our siblings and extended family all heard it. He was humble and he was humorous as he progressed.

His disease took a toll on him, and I watched him vanish before my eyes. His children saw their fun-loving dad who was a college football player diminish into one you couldn't recognize.

He did manage to take a trip with his entire family as his last wish. He even got on the trails with them for a bit. They are a very outdoors family—hiking was what they did.

The week after they were home, he had an appointment the next morning to get the dreaded tube down his throat. He didn't want that; he wanted to go in peace and with dignity. But he was conflicted because he felt his children wanted that.

He had to sleep on the couch downstairs because he couldn't walk and no one could carry him up the stairs. He passed on that night.

His family are all grown now, with their own families. All men and women of God. He was my angel on earth and he led me to the Lord through his gentle actions and loving demeanor.

ALS took away my brother's physical life, but nothing will take away my brother's spiritual life.

FINAL THOUGHTS

You, too, can Be Amazing!

I hope this book has renewed your thought process, and I encourage you to read it over and over again. I'm not a master of all of this, just a student, still learning, still growing. In fact, I don't plan on retiring from this EVER. The word *retire* just makes me tired!

My challenge for you is to apply all of these principles and watch your life start to shift. Not only will you have an amazing life but you, too, can Be Amazing!

In the words of John Maxwell, "Forget the motivation trap. DO IT NOW!"

ABOUT THE AUTHOR

TINA BLACK had a successful career for 18 years as a dental hygienist, but her husband Bryan Black saw so much more potential in her and knew she was destined to do great things for people and the world. In April 1998, they purchased Great Lakes Academy of Hair Design in Port Huron, Michigan, and Tina decided to become a cosmetologist. After completing the program at her own school, she became an instructor there. When she received a flyer about joining the Paul Mitchell Schools network, she jumped at the opportunity and immediately flew out to meet the company's dean and cofounder, Winn Claybaugh. Tina loved what she heard and her school became Paul Mitchell The School Great Lakes, one of the first ten Paul Mitchell Schools.

Tina also owned a salon from 1999 to 2006, including two years with internationally renowned salon owner, celebrity stylist, and educator Kelly Cardenas, her longtime mentor. Among other things, Kelly taught Tina how to teach her staff and students to become financially independent. In January 2015, Tina and her daughter Brianna Black became co-owners of a Ken Paves Salon, partnering with one of the most sought-after hairstylists in the entertainment and fashion industries.

Knowing she wanted to do more and inspire more future professionals, Tina opened a second school in 2006: Paul Mitchell The School Michigan, in Sterling Heights, Michigan. She wore many hats at that school, including learning leader, motivational speaker, success coach, education leader, and dream maker. Tina also serves as a partner appraisal leader (PAL), mentoring other school owners in the Paul Mitchell Schools network. Inspired by the book *Be Nice (Or Else!)* by Winn Claybaugh, Tina and her school director, Shaun

Chiodo, developed a student-run program called the Be Nice Team; the concept has spread to all Paul Mitchell Schools. Tina also worked closely with Dr. Susan Swearer, Professor of School Psychology for the University of Nebraska–Lincoln, to write the N-Lighten self-empowerment and anti-bullying curriculum for all Paul Mitchell Schools.

Tina is heavily involved in the Paul Mitchell Schools' annual FUNraising Campaign, which has raised millions of dollars for organizations like Cancer Schmancer, Food 4 Africa, Morris Animal Foundation, and Children's Miracle Network Hospitals, to name just a few. Tina's schools routinely rank in the top 10 fundraising schools, out of more than 100 Paul Mitchell Schools nationwide. She also serves on the board of directors for the nonprofit Andrew Gomez Dream Foundation.

Under Tina's leadership, her two Michigan schools have won many awards within the Paul Mitchell Schools network for leadership, culture, facilities (best Wash House and Color Bar), and best store front, to name a few. She has now branched out to Florida, where she opened Paul Mitchell The School Fort Myers in 2011. She plans to open more Paul Mitchell Schools and Ken Paves salons.

Tina has spent countless hours becoming the leader and mentor she is today. She is a John Maxwell Team Certified Coach and was personally coached for many years by Mary Burlingame, director of coaching for Paul Mitchell Advanced Education. Tina is a keynote speaker on leadership for many organizations such as Compass, Chamber of Commerce, local businesses, salons, hair shows, and nonprofits. Her topics include Get Your Leadership

On, Leading the Next Generation of Leaders, What Your Boss Won't Tell You, and more. Tina and her business partner Shaun Chiodo lead online salon mastermind groups to train salon owners and managers on business and leadership principles.

Tina's passion to make the world a better place has led her to mission trips in Guatemala with the John Maxwell Team, where she helped to train over 25,000 leaders in all sectors of leadership. She plans to continue traveling with the team in other countries as opportunities arise.

Along with other authors and speakers, Tina is currently developing the Detroit Leadership Initiative Team to train small business owners on leadership, and she dreams of starting a next-generation Compass leadership networking team, to inspire and train the millennial generation and prepare them for the workforce. With her passion for helping people see their true potential and reach greatness, Tina will continue to open schools and mentor and motivate everyone she meets.

For more information and to subscribe to Tina's Desk weekly leadership messages, visit www.TinaBlack.net.